IN THE FOOTSTEPS OF GREY OWL

JOURNEY INTO THE ANCIENT FOREST

GARY AND JOANIE McGUFFIN

National Library of Canada Cataloguing in Publication

McGuffin, Gary
      In the footsteps of Grey Owl : journey into the ancient forest / by Gary and Joanie McGuffin.

ISBN 0-7710-5537-4

1. Ontario, Northern–Description and travel. 2. Canoes and canoeing–Ontario, Northern. I. McGuffin, Joanie. II. Title.

FC3094.4.M32 2002   917.13'13044   C2002-902697-0
F1059.N67M32 2002

We acknowledge the financial support of the Government of Canada through the Book Publishing Industry Development Program for our publishing activities. We further acknowledge the support of the Canada Council for the Arts and the Ontario Arts Council for our publishing program.

Grey Owl quotations are taken from *The Men of the Last Fontier* (Laurentian Library edition, 1976; Toronto: The Macmillan Company of Canada Limited, 1931), *Pilgrims of the Wild* (Laurentian Library edition, 1978; Toronto: Macmillan Canada, 1934), *The Adventures of Sajo and Her Beaver People* (London: Lovat Dickson & Thompson, 1935), and *Tales of an Empty Cabin* (Stoddart paperback ed., 1992; Toronto: Macmillan Canada, 1936).

Book design by K.T. Njo
Grey Owl photo courtesy Glenbow Archives NA-4868-211
All other photographs by Gary McGuffin
Map by Visutronx

Title-page image: White pine along the Lady Evelyn River.
Image on pages 10-11: Ridges of white pine at sunrise. Temagami.
Image on pages 44-45: Fog in the valleys at sunset. Algoma Highlands.

Typeset in Bembo by M&S, Toronto
Printed and bound in Canada
This book is printed on totally chlorine-free paper. For information about chlorine-free products go to <www.chlorinefreeproducts.org>.

McClelland & Stewart Ltd.
The Canadian Publishers
481 University Avenue
Toronto, Ontario
M5G 2E9
www.mcclelland.com

1   2   3   4   5   06   05   04   03   02

To Sila, our daughter, and Kalija, our faithful canine companion

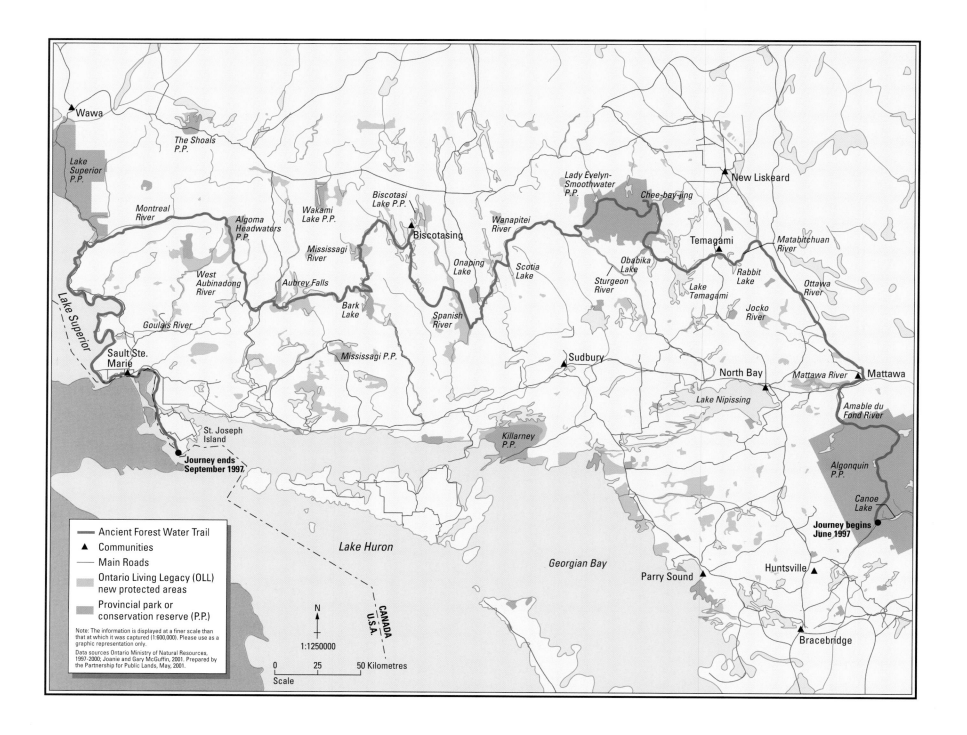

Wawa

The Shoals
P.P.

Lake
Superior
P.P.

Montreal
River

Algoma
Headwaters
P.P.

Wakami
Lake P.P.

Biscotasi
Lake P.P.

Lady Evelyn-
Smoothwater
P.P.

New Liskeard

Chee-bay-jing

West
Aubinadong
River

Mississagi
River

Wanapitei
River

Biscotasing

Temagami

Matabitchuan
River

Aubrey Falls

Onaping
Lake

Scotia
Lake

Obabika
Lake

Rabbit
Lake

Goulais River

Bark
Lake

Spanish
River

Sturgeon
River

Lake
Temagami

Jocko
River

Ottawa
River

Lake Superior

Sault Ste.
Marie

Mississagi P.P.

Sudbury

North Bay

Mattawa River

Mattawa

St. Joseph
Island

Lake Nipissing

Amable du
Fond River

Journey ends
September 1997

Killarney
P.P.

Algonquin
P.P.

Lake Huron

Canoe
Lake

Journey begins
June 1997

Georgian Bay

Huntsville

Parry Sound

Bracebridge

Ancient Forest Water Trail

▲ Communities

Main Roads

Ontario Living Legacy (OLL)
new protected areas

Provincial park or
conservation reserve (P.P.)

Note: The information is displayed at a finer scale than
that at which it was captured (1:600,000). Please use as a
graphic representation only.

Data sources Ontario Ministry of Natural Resources,
1997-2000; Joanie and Gary McGuffin, 2001. Prepared by
the Partnership for Public Lands, May, 2001.

N

CANADA
U.S.A.

1:1250000

0   25   50 Kilometres

Scale

CONTENTS

Paddling into a brewing summer storm. MacPherson Lake.

I've always been instinctively suspicious of those environmental advocates who rarely connect with what they're trying to save. Perhaps if you spend too much time staring at a computer monitor, or frequenting airports, conferences, and downtown offices, you lose sight of the larger picture.

Well, in the pages ahead get ready to walk in the footsteps of Grey Owl and to be reminded of what it's all about. Paddle with Gary and Joanie McGuffin "in the shade of huge pines." Feel "how water moves around rock, how wind moves around islands." And breathe the cool night air, as billions of stars "spill down into the lake."

Thank you, Gary and Joanie. Because if *this* is what's at stake, I can easily endure one more long-winded meeting. In fact, bring on many *more*!

The McGuffins' journey into the ancient forest served the purpose of connecting nature's magnificent reality out there, on-the-ground, to a crucial but more distant provincial negotiation regarding its future. This planning process, confined largely to meeting rooms, was called Lands for Life. Gary and Joanie's goal was to "become a catalyst for self-education, understanding, and appreciation for the forests, the waterways flowing through them, and the animal and plant life inhabiting them."

In the end, Lands for Life produced a "Living Legacy" of 378 new or expanded parks and other protected areas that totalled more than six million acres, including large chunks of our authors' cherished homeplace – the Algoma Highlands. This was by far the most important single decision to protect nature ever taken in Ontario, and the McGuffins were a big part of the team that made it possible.

Given their history, I hope the McGuffin clan's travels will predict future conservation success stories. Let's see: last summer they were exploring Lake Superior's North Shore islands. That's great news, because these islands are slated for inclusion in a spectacular, yet-to-be-announced National Marine Conservation Area. And this summer? Oh good . . . the McGuffins are paddling 3,000 kilometres in a 21-foot cedar-strip canoe from the Pigeon River on Lake Superior to the Severn River on Georgian Bay, which just happens to be the same geography being planned as a Heritage Coastline.

I think I see a pattern emerging here: Gary and Joanie McGuffin's journeys have moved beyond their original goal of catalyst, to that of lifeline to the wild. And not a moment too soon.

Monte Hummel
President, World Wildlife Fund Canada
June 2002

THE JOURNEY IN WORDS

For black bear cubs, the furrowed bark of an ancient white pine is a ladder to the safety among the tree's strong limbs. Apex Lake.

IN THE BEGINNING

One week after Gary was born, a small package arrived postmarked Temagami, Ontario. Inside, his mother found a carefully wrapped silver spoon engraved with Gary's name and birthdate on one side and the word "Freedom" on the other. The gift was from Mr. McLean, the elderly prospector whose cabin was situated only a stone's throw from the family's summer camp. The following summer, Gary had his first ride in Mr. McLean's handmade cedar canvas canoe across the waters of Rabbit Lake. Over the years, visits with Mr. McLean often happened on the grey days when the spruce branches hung heavy with a steady downpour. Gary and his father would set forth on the trail to Mr. McLean's cabin bearing two buckets of spring water and a loaf of warm-from-the-oven bread. The prospector would greet them with mugs of piping-hot tea and a generous flow of news ranging from the weather to fishing and the general health of the forest. Mr. McLean would also tell stories about his eighty-year life spent travelling and working around the world, from helping to build the Suez Canal to sailing ships around Cape Horn. But what intrigued Gary more than anything was the prospector's life in northern Ontario. Apart from prospecting, Mr. McLean had been a teacher in the local public school. His shelves were lined with books about adventure and the North. Among them were Grey Owl's *Tales of an Empty Cabin*, *The Men of the Last Frontier*, *The Adventures of Sajo and Her Beaver People*, and *Pilgrims of the Wild*.

Grey Owl (born Archie Stansfeld Belaney in 1888 in Hastings, Sussex) and Mr. McLean had both been shaped by a life of living on the land in the Temagami region from the early 1900s until 1914, when they both went off to war. Upon Grey Owl's return to Temagami as a wounded soldier, he grew embittered by a new era of men who had moved into the forest causing wholesale destruction. They cut timber fast and furious, and trapped the beavers and other fur-bearers almost to extinction. In 1925, Grey Owl met a beautiful, young Iroquois woman named Anahareo, with whom he fell in love. Anahareo's influence on Grey Owl led him to give up trapping and commit his life to the preservation of the "beaver people" and the conservation of wilderness. His hugely popular books and his famous public-speaking tours of the 1930s described the forest and its inhabitants in a way that is as relevant today as it was seventy years ago. On those rainy afternoons when it was just Gary and Mr. McLean, the old prospector would open Grey Owl's books and read aloud to his student of the forest.

During the summers, Mr. McLean and Gary paddled to many places; they even had a "special spot" that not many people knew of, a place where the white pines were huge and the ground was thick and spongy with fallen needles. The ravens soaring above the treetops were only specks in the sky. This was a sacred place, Mr. McLean explained, where the people of this land years ago brought their elders when they were ready to enter the spirit world.

Most memorable to Gary was paddling in the shade of those huge pines, walking up to their mammoth flanks, feeling the deep grooves in their bark, breathing in the sharp smell of pine pitch. Lying supine on the forest floor, Gary and Mr. McLean would stare up into the place where the uppermost branches seemed to hold up the sky and listen to the hush of billions of pine needles being strummed by the wind.

◄◦►

My parents built a cottage on the Muskoka Lakes north of Toronto when I was four years old. We spent many happy summers exploring nature by way of the forest trails on foot and by canoe, rowboat, or sailboat through the lakes. We used to drive to the cottage at night and make the three-kilometre crossing of Lake Joseph from the landing in the dark. Sometimes it was so dark my father would navigate almost solely by the compass. I would sit in the back of the boat with my sister and my brother looking up at the stars.

Many times throughout the summers, I would escape by canoe in the evening to float on the bay beneath the billions of stars. The sparkling heavens would spill down into the lake and the reflected surface became another universe. I imagined myself paddling across the sky in my magic canoe. I could see the dark shoreline with its beautiful silhouetted shapes of pine and cedar and spruce, and I could smell the musky, sweet odours of earth and flowers and cedar in the night air.

I especially liked the beginning of summer holidays when time stretched out long and lovely in the days ahead. I would go into the forest and listen to the birds: the white-throated sparrow with its clear, crisp notes, the ovenbird and the thrushes and songbirds. I loved them all and always carried binoculars around my neck so I could observe without disturbing them. Sometimes I would watch the beavers at their dam, or a heron stalking the shallows or a turtle sunning itself on the rocks. Everywhere I looked, things were alive and moving, but I could scarcely believe how quietly they all went about their business. Were humans ever as quiet? It was so noisy in the city where I came from. Summers were soft and gentle. There was time to explore and swim, and to read in the hammock that swung beneath the hemlocks. This is where I first met Grey Owl. I would read his books while listening to the lapping of the water by the shore.

THE ALGOMA HIGHLANDS

Several years ago, we spent a whole summer canoeing around the world's largest expanse of freshwater, Lake Superior. During our trip, we discovered more than 3,200 kilometres (2,000 miles) of shoreline shaped by fire and ice. This watershed of rivers and forests inspired numerous journeys in all seasons. In particular, we became fascinated with the headwaters of four rivers – the Goulais, Batchawana, Chippewa, and Montreal, which all flow into the east side of Lake Superior from the Algoma Highlands.

When the last ice age retreated ten thousand years ago, the vegetation was subarctic, as it is today on the tundra where plants grow slowly hugging the ground. With the climate warming, vegetation grew luxuriant and ever higher around the fresh-water lakes and rivers. The Great Lakes–St. Lawrence Forest eventually emerged, an unbroken wilderness of conifers and deciduous species covering a vast area from the northern Appalachians to Lake Superior, from the Mississippi to the Atlantic coast. A squirrel could travel hundreds of kilometres without touching the forest floor. But the descriptive feature of the Algoma Highlands forest that attracted us most was the majestic white pine that cloaked ridge upon ridge. We planned our trip that winter and set off the following spring canoeing and camping our way into and through the Algoma Highlands.

The ice had only just vanished, and the spring green of tiny buds and baby leaves cast a spell on us. Our footprints joined those of fresh moose and black bear tracks in the high-water mark's soft mud flats. Narrow creeks and bubbling streams danced with speckled trout. Pine marten, mink, otter, and beaver had all left their markings along the way. Old portage blazes revealed footpaths most recently used by a large timber wolf. Colourful warblers returning from South and Central America had flown back to nest in the tops of the great pines. This was a forest that had been evolving largely undisturbed for a long time. This complex and irreplaceable forest now covered less than 1 per cent of its range prior to European contact. The current forestry plans detailed how this particular place was going to be cut. We desperately wanted to do something to save it. How could we make people aware of the Highlands and raise enough public support to prevent losing yet one more of Earth's special places?

An idea began to take shape one day as we stood on top of a ridge overlooking Gord Lake. Magnificent centuries-old pine stretched out before us. We would paddle a route across Ontario from the places of our childhood summers all the way to the Algoma Highlands, the very route that Grey Owl traversed in his wanderings between Lake Temagami and the Mississagi River. Our idea was to create an adventure story through which people could learn about the complete forest landscape and realize how fast the roadless, self-sustaining wilderness Grey Owl described seventy years ago was disappearing. We could be a voice for the forest and its inhabitants.

THE PLAN UNFOLDS

Once we had made our commitment to the voyage, plans began to take shape. The departure date was spring 1997, and in the twelve months prior, we were kept busy finalizing all the details. We acquired topographic maps and began research to decide upon our route. We wrote letters to various companies and organizations and contacted the three major environmental groups in Ontario: the Federation of Ontario Naturalists, the Wildlands League, and World Wildlife Fund Canada. We discovered that our timing for the journey could not have been better. In 1996, the Ontario provincial government was planning to decide once and for all where industrial and recreational uses would take place, and what wilderness, wildlife, and natural heritage features would be preserved in the forty-six-million-hectare area of central and northern Ontario. The environmental organizations considered the matter of such importance that they formed an alliance called the Partnership for Public Lands. The alliance would pool resources and present a strong, united front while participating in the decision-making process.

In 1989, World Wildlife Fund Canada launched The Endangered Spaces Campaign under the signatures of all the provincial and territorial premiers. The goal of the campaign was simple: to ensure that all of Canada's natural regions would be represented in a network of protected areas by the year 2000. We were planning to paddle through as many of the prime candidates for protection in the Great Lakes-St. Lawrence Forest landscape as possible. It would be invaluable for us to direct the public's attention to the Partnership's campaign. Somehow we had to help move people's hearts and minds to take action and get involved with their voices and their votes.

We talked to a variety of forestry research scientists and began to sketch out where the best examples of this Great Lakes-St. Lawrence Forest could be found between the Ottawa Valley and Lake Superior. During this time, we met forest physiological geneticist George Buchert, who specialized in old-growth white pine. In his quiet but passionate way, he described how the traditional harvesting of white pine had greatly depleted the gene pool. Old-growth white pine needs an abundance of their kind for cross-pollination to maintain the strength of the species. As well, it takes more than one hundred years to grow a white pine to harvestable size. It is far easier and more profitable for the forest companies to replant cutover lands with red pine.

We had also heard about two forest scientists who had done a number of on-ground old-growth forest studies across northern Ontario from the Spanish River to Algonquin Provincial Park. Quite by coincidence one day at the put-in launch near our cabin on Rabbit Lake, we were hailed by name by two men who turned out to be these very scientists. They introduced themselves as Peter Quinby and Tom Lee. For several hours we swatted blackflies and discussed the preservation of Ontario's ancient forests. They explained the work of their organization, Ancient Forest Exploration and Research. We discovered they

had been carrying out their studies with Earthwatch Institute for the past two years in a location just north of our cabin.

We talked of our plans to retrace the trails of Grey Owl across northern Ontario and find the special forests he so eloquently described in his books. Then Peter and Tom shared their idea with us. They hoped that a recognized recreational corridor could be created to link together the remaining ancient forests of the Great Lakes-St. Lawrence region all the way from Algonquin Provincial Park to the shores of Lake Superior. They had already sketched out a possible route. That was when our 1,900-kilometre (1,200-mile) journey to save the ancient forests was born.

◄◦►

Simply exploring the route that linked together the last remaining islands of the Great Lakes-St. Lawrence old-growth forest left in North America was a goal of ours. However, we wanted our journey to have an immediate and positive impact. We wanted to share our adventures with people in real-time from the wilderness such as we had done via CBC Radio on two previous treks across Canada by canoe and bicycle. We hoped that our trip could become a catalyst for self-education, understanding, and appreciation for these forests, the waterways flowing through them, and the animal and plant life inhabiting them. We wanted to inspire others to undertake their own trips into Ontario's ancient forests. Our big problem was how to communicate along a route where there were very few telephones!

Fortunately, the development of satellite communication was flourishing in 1997, as was widespread Internet use with Web site development and e-mail correspondence. The companies whose equipment we needed were only too eager to prove their products on an exciting and publicized voyage. What better way to demonstrate the ease and abilities of digital photography, satellite communication, and powerful laptop computers than on a remote northern canoe trip? In the months leading up to our journey, we acquired a specialized communications system and, most necessary, the array of two solar panels, a 140-watt inverter, and a gel cell 12-volt battery that would power the system with the sun's energy. This equipment would enable us to phone in weekly to CBC Radio, provide weekly colour features for Southam News, and keep a daily journal and photo album on a Web site.

Of course, there was also the low-tech side to our trip, which was really more important to consider. We felt the thrill of a journey becoming reality on the day our red canoe arrived. The canoe's evolution is rooted in the aboriginal people's need

The communications system we carried for 1,900 kilometres across 130 portages to broadcast our story of the ancient forest to CBC Radio, our Web site, <www.adventurers.org>, and the fifty-seven Southam newspapers across Canada. We are surrounded here by the fifteen newspaper articles that appeared in the Saturday edition of the Sault Star.

to navigate a landscape of rivers and lakes, and was the single most important piece of our equipment. Our canoe weighed 25 kilograms (55 pounds), reasonable for a single-person carry, although the 5.6-metre (18.5-foot) length might prove a little unwieldy in the wind, or across an overgrown portage. A 45-kilogram (100-pound) waterproof case containing the delicate communications equipment fit amidships by a hair's breadth. This felt like a puzzle starting to fit together.

The specialized high-resolution digital camera arrived two days before our scheduled departure, which was the first week of June 1997. We tested the system by downloading some photos into the laptop and sending them off into space. Filled with both excitement and trepidation, we waited to see if the images would make the 32,000-kilometre (20,000-mile) trek to the satellite and back to the receiving dish in Ottawa, where the images would enter the telephone lines and arrive in our webulator's computer. Success! With the last puzzle piece fitting into place, all gear and canoe loaded, Gary, Kalija (our Alaskan Malamute), and I were ready for our journey.

IN THE FOOTSTEPS OF GREY OWL

It was early June when we packed the canoe on the shores of Canoe Lake in Algonquin Provincial Park. Three packs containing food, camping gear, and clothing, and two waterproof cases containing cameras, film, and the communications equipment were fitted neatly into the centre space beneath the gunwales with just enough room for Kalija to nestle in behind my bow seat. We pushed off from shore, letting the canoe glide out across the water. Those first paddle strokes were thrilling and made the journey a reality for us. We turned to wave once more to my parents and our friends who had come to see us off. The excitement and support of both our parents made each new venture in our lives part of their lives too.

◄○►

Early in the journey, we met up with two long-time friends on a portage trail heading north into Burntroot Lake. We had discussed months ago of paddling the "Algonquin Park" leg of our route together but had been unable to commit to an exact departure date and had abandoned the idea. It was a delightful coincidence, and we welcomed the camaraderie to laugh with us over our aching muscles. While gathered about our small fire that first evening together beneath the pines, sipping tea and eating warm cinnamon buns, not one of us wanted to break the deep, relaxing silence. A barred owl called in the distance. Gary mimicked it, making a sound like "Who cooks for you, who cooks for you, who cooks for you all." It grew nearer. Moments later, the owl arrived on silent wings to claim the treetops overhead as his territory. Another barred owl joined the excitement, and a terrific racket ensued overhead as the two owls sparred, sounding like enraged chimpanzees.

Suddenly a full forest orchestra touched off; the yodel of loons, the shrill soprano of spring peepers, the deep bass of bullfrogs, a two-note see-saw of the saw-whet owl, and one pure sweet solo of a white-throated sparrow. Then a haunting music rose beneath it all to fill the moonlit night, the yipping and howling of Eastern timber wolves.

The great irony of Algonquin Provincial Park is that although it is Ontario's oldest protected wilderness area, it was established to protect the timber supply for industry. By the late 1800s, the timber barons had all but exhausted the Ottawa Valley of its great white pine to supply the demands of the

Knee-deep in the muck of a boggy portage while crossing the height of land lakes from the Sturgeon River to the Wanapitei River.

British navy. It was realized that if some measure of protection for the species was not taken, it would all be gone. And so the park was formed in 1893 and has been both a tourist mecca and a timber supply ever since. A century of logging is evident everywhere from logging chutes to logging camps. Today, machines operate throughout much of the year cutting and hauling logs out of the park on a vast system of permanent roads. There are enough kilometres of roads throughout the park that if threaded end to end in a straight line, they would take you from Algonquin all the way to Florida!

At a picturesque waterfall along the upper Petawawa River, we lined our canoe down an old logging chute, being careful to avoid any dangerous spikes. Some kilometres later we discovered the remains of the Barnet Farm Depot, which was established in 1882 at the south end of Burntroot Lake to provide supplies to the nearby logging camps. Foundations of huge square timbers and rocks now protruded from the long grass where willows, stinging nettle, elderberries, and other sun-loving plants grew in happy abandon. Hidden amongst the shoreline shrubbery, we found a dilapidated "Alligator," an amphibious self-propelled craft that was used to tow log booms and winch rafts of logs overland from lake to lake. There were small reminders of the women who lived here, like a narrow leather boot sole fringed with tiny nails. Several names popped to mind as I pondered this piece of footwear: Elizabeth du Fond, wife of Amable du Fond, whose namesake river was at the northern edge of the park; Mrs. Taylor Statton, who managed the well-known Taylor Statton Camps still in operation on Canoe Lake; and Molly Colson, a nurse who managed the park's first hotel along the Grand Trunk Railway.

Though our route through the park via Big Trout, Burntroot, Perley, Catfish, Cedar, and Kioshkokwi lakes is one of the most popular, we never saw another soul save our two friends. We followed the shoreline closely rather than travelling point to point, portage to portage, as many paddlers are apt to do in their haste to reach the next campsite. Great thick cedar trunks spiralled out from shore like unicorn horns. The bases of their solid trunks required two people to give them a "hug." Individual ancient white pines that missed the logger's axe waved their feathered limbs at a height that was twice that of the surrounding forest canopy. Time and again in the distance, huge stumps and root systems remaining from the early logging days fooled us into thinking they were moose. We saw old pine trees that had fallen near shore lying submerged in an underwater world where perch darted between the limbs on which birds once nested.

◄o►

Southwest winds, a violent rainstorm that turned suddenly to hail, northern lights, and then finally freshening winds from the northwest set the tone of varied weather in our first week on the route. One afternoon we stopped for lunch at a small island on Catfish Lake. We settled down among a patch of plump red cranberries that had wintered over from the previous fall. Blue herons criss-crossed the sky on wide wings while others hunted in the shallows, striking with precision into the swirling schools of minnows. Later, to our delight, we discovered a young bull moose munching on the cranberries on the other side of the island, enjoying them as much as we had. A quick scan of the wetland with binoculars revealed moose in every direction. We counted five bulls with velvet racks of antlers, a cow with her twin calves, and a young moose and an older, greyer one feeding together.

We paddled over to watch the cow moose with her calves. She dipped her head in the lake, ripping up arrowhead roots

At the confluence of the Aubinadong and West Aubinadong rivers, we made camp on one of the many gravel bars.

while her calves pressed tightly to the cover of shore. The cow was aware of us, but she tolerated our presence as long as we kept our distance. This was her home: her kitchen, her bedroom, the birthplace of her calves. Even travelling by canoe, we always felt our human presence was known. A snapping turtle sunning on a flat rock suddenly hurled itself into the lake as we slipped by. Before we ever saw them, the sound of scrambling claws confirmed that a mother bear was sending her cubs to safety up a giant white pine. Otters interrupted their joyful bank-sliding as we came into view. A beaver circled, slapping its tail. At day's end when the light faded, our intrusion on the landscape seemed less profound. The loons, wolves, and owls responded to our calls and we felt in tune with another meaning of home.

At Kiosk campground, once a small mill town on the north edge of the park, we portaged the dam leaving Algonquin to descend the Amable du Fond River. This river had once been a travel and trade route between Georgian Bay and the Ottawa Valley. Evening was upon us, yet we could not find a place to make camp. Alders and black ash pressed in from either side, forming a tangled jungle of impenetrable vegetation. Ahead the meandering Amable du Fond River was about to drop off into the unseen roar of a second mighty gorge. Just then we noticed a yellow portage sign placed at the brink of the falls. We pulled ashore and followed the freshly mowed portage path up to a beautiful log cabin. The path continued on past it and down to the base of the gorge, but we dropped the packs to admire the view. Sunny yellow coreopsis, purple bellflowers, delphiniums, and wild roses grew in profusion about the house in rockery beds, over trellises, in baskets and pots. Behind the house was a small barn and a paddock, where, much to Kalija's delight, two fine Belgian horses resided. Dozens of white canoes piled neatly

on racks attracted us to inquire within about a place to set up our tent for the night.

A man appeared on the porch, hailing us with a hearty "Hi, McGuffins! I was just looking you up on the Internet and here you are portaging through my garden." Surprised, Gary replied with a laugh, "That's virtual reality for you!" Lynda and Ian Kovacs, along with their two daughters, Becky and Sarah, operated Halfway Chute Outfitters equipping canoeists for trips into Algonquin Park and along the Mattawa River. Ian had brushed off the trail and put out the park portage sign when he began following our journey. We were, they informed us, the annual quota of paddlers that they see descending this river.

They lit us a fire, filled our water bottles, and, after we had made a quick supper, they invited us in for tea. The Kovacs had been residents of the lumber mill town of Kiosk in the late 1970s. Over the course of five years using all their holidays and weekends, they had built their own home.

Growing up with an outfitting business, Becky and Sarah had had the opportunity of seeing their northern Ontario home from a different point of view. Visitors to the park arrived from all across the globe to rent canoes for a "true Canadian experience" of a wilderness canoe trip in Algonquin. They were constantly commenting to Becky and Sarah of how lucky they were living among beautiful forests and clean rivers and lakes.

The contours on our topographic map clearly revealed that in its 40-kilometre (25-mile) length between Kioshkokwi Lake downstream to the Mattawa, the waterway drops 155 metres (510 feet). Most of the whitewater lay from this point to the Eau Claire Gorge. Negotiating the dangerous low-water rapids was a big challenge in our heavily laden, lengthy canoe. Avoiding the visible and invisible sharp black rocks was nerve-racking. Nine hours later, we finally arrived at the brink of Eau

Claire Gorge and set the tent amidst the tall, fragrant ferns. We turned the canoe over and surveyed the battle scars etched forever into the red gelcoat of the canoe's once-gleaming hull. After making bushwhack portages, our arms and legs looked nearly as wartorn, but a quick swim washed away the dried blood and cooled the bug bites. We were refreshed and ready for tomorrow.

The kilometre hike around the Eau Claire Gorge over bedrock, under pine, and with numerous lookouts along the gorge proved spectacular. Downstream, the river slowed into a series of small sun-dappled lakes: Smith, Crooked Chute, and Moore. The hills receded. We felt our heart rates slow with the river pace. For another day we paddled north to complete the river link between Algonquin and the Mattawa. The humidity was high. Yellow pollen wafted from the pines like smoke. Kalija panted and we sneezed, heaving the unbearably heavy packs around the lip of Horse Race Rapids. Cedar waxwings twittered and kingfishers chattered, while muskrats slipped noiselessly in and out of the water.

◄○►

Steel grey thunderclouds rolled down the Mattawa's historic valley as we left the Amable du Fond and turned downstream to run the Rapides Campion near Samuel de Champlain Provincial Park. Fourteen years ago, we canoed this Canadian Heritage River upstream on our way across Canada to the Beaufort Sea. Once again we felt part of the river's six-thousand-year-old role of providing a waterway link between the Ottawa Valley and the Upper Great Lakes. Aboriginal peoples travelled the Mattawa, later guiding the explorers and fur traders. Along the eighteenth-century fur trade express route between Montreal and Lake Superior's Grand Portage, the Mattawa

River proved to be one of the most challenging sections with its rugged portages that remain in much the same condition today. As we hoisted up loads less than half the weight of the voyageurs, and negotiated the rocks and mud along the trails, the symbolic white crosses placed high above the river were a poignant reminder to us of those perilous days when even a minor medical trauma could be fatal.

We arrived in Mattawa, located at the confluence of the Mattawa and Ottawa rivers, feeling tired and hungry. Our first food package had dwindled to a few tea bags, a spoonful of honey, and a package of soup, and Kalija was all out of her dry kibble. We had arranged to pick up the first of six prepackaged food and film caches at the Tourism Centre. We had been two weeks on the trail now and so we appreciated a day off to reorganize, repack, do a washing, get a restaurant meal, catch up on the Web site journal, and send a newspaper story. We walked the streets admiring the huge, colourful murals adorning the sides of buildings.

◄○►

There was a grand feeling of arriving in open space as we canoed out onto the Ottawa River. This body of water, reminiscent of a Norwegian fjord, forms the boundary between the provinces of Ontario and Quebec. Since the Ontario shore with its small islands and bays gave some protection from the possible northwest winds, it appeared more hospitable to us than the Quebec shore with its dramatic sweep of endless cliffs. The loons delighted in answering their own voices in this incredible valley of echoes.

The geology and geography of the valley was as it had been for several thousand years. But the forest that existed here two hundred years ago, a magnificent corridor of massive white pine, shall never be seen again. The remaining ancient pine that grew in scattered, inaccessible bands along the cliffs were testimony to the size of the timber we had seen in turn-of-the-century black-and-white photographs of logging on the Ottawa River. No other tree was anywhere near as tall, straight, and strong as the white pine. King of the forest, the white pine surpasses the height of ten-storey buildings. Despite their impressive size, these abundant trees were vulnerable in their abundance beside this perfect transportation corridor to the Atlantic Ocean. The great white pine soon became a timber supply for a young and growing nation.

The clay banks at Grand Campment Bay along the Ottawa River were in a state of constant erosion with the unnatural surges in water level. Brown sediment hung in suspension so thick that our paddle blades disappeared from view within inches of the surface. The afternoon we stopped it was so windy that we decided to go for a hike up into the Owain Forest, a place Gary had known since boyhood. We filled our bottles with filtered water from Owain Creek and followed a familiar trail up from the Ottawa River into the heart of the Owain Forest. The trail wound through yellow birch and black ash forest, some hardwood sugar maple and dominant stands of mature red and white pine, then passed through a green tunnel of willows. At the top of the trail, we pushed back the wild honeysuckle and royal ferns, and our paradise dissolved. The sound of woodpeckers, thrushes, and our own voices echoed eerily in the scarred clearing. A recent and very controversial logging operation had pushed another road into the Temagami wilderness, taking more than its world-renowned pine. Seedlings had been planted, but even if a tenth of them survived, these tiny trees could never replace a forest that had evolved into the beautiful park-like setting that visitors worldwide would have

paid handsomely to experience. The greatest losers were all the species that called this forest home. The complexity of interrelationships between species living within a roadless place of any extensive size cannot be reproduced. The hunting and fishing pressures increase with accessibility and the very nature of the forest mosaic alters as the deep forest-dwellers are pushed out by the creatures who have adapted to open space at the edge of clearcuts and roads. The original forest has been reduced to isolated islands in a sea of human-altered landscapes. In Canada, there is a tendency to believe in the illusion of a wilderness that goes on forever, but it is time to take responsibility for rejuvenating the landscape we have already harvested from and let all that is still wild and without roads remain that way. We hoped fervently that people would react and speak out before it was too late.

◄o►

Ducks everywhere were with families. A brightly coloured wood duck burst out from its cliffside nest leaving five newly hatched chicks clustered nervously on a patch of moss. Another time, I mistook a flurry of two dozen flightless merganser chicks for a small rapid until, confused by our approach, the group split in all directions. It is always funny watching merganser families passing one another. The youngsters in tow show no allegiance to a particular mother, as they will often turn and follow the other group. As we came ashore on an island one evening, we discovered some ducks were still nesting. Kalija poked her nose under a clump of cedar, flushing a teal duck off her ground-level nest. Catching a glimpse of the creamy white eggs, we quickly packed up and found a more suitable campsite.

We left the Ottawa behind us at the Matabitchuan River, or "Waw-bos Nah-mat-ah-bee." This was home turf for Gary.

Between here and Rabbit Lake, he knew the country intimately. For eighteen years, he had spent his summers here. The cabin Gary built when he was sixteen had been our first home. I had travelled with him many times on dark nights when it was only the faintest outline of hills or the sound of the creeks and the distance between them that led us home by ski or canoe. I'm sure Gary could have found his way home blindfolded. This land held good memories of paddling canoes, exploring old forests, catching pickerel, walking the forest trails, and picking blueberries.

At the river mouth, we paddled over the place where a fur trading post once stood before the dam drowned the lower Matabitchuan. Then came the steep portage up into Fourbass Lake that put us 105 metres (350 feet) above the Ottawa River with an expansive view to the north, east, and south. We balanced along the edge of an old log flume where millions of board feet of pine were once sluiced down to the Ottawa River. We climbed amongst the drift logs heaped up in a mound of what looked like bleached bones. Recently the Fourbass Lake headpond had been lowered 8 metres (27 feet) for dam repairs, revealing a shoreline that had long been covered in water. An archeological dig unearthed clay pipes and a wheeled cart, which confirmed the notion of a cart track that was once thought to exist between Fourbass and the Montreal River. Blue flag irises, wild roses, and sheep laurel were blooming in profusion along the shores of this picturesque lake of rocky outcroppings and magnificent flatrock campsites. One great pine left standing dead following a forest fire years ago held a huge stick nest reminiscent of a Dr. Seuss drawing. For as long as Gary could remember, the osprey and their nest had been here. We watched as three osprey circled, dipped, and dove in the turbulent winds above us.

The Matabitchuan spilled out from between the huge blocks of dark granite and the angular sheet of bedrock flanking it. On one slab of rock, we found a small red ochre figure of a moose. The physical remnants of human history are always so riveting. A pictograph, a pottery shard, a spearpoint pondered within the context of its surroundings is a journey in itself, taking one back down the corridor of time. We think, as we observe this small red drawing, what of the weather, the wind, the sunrise and sunset that day when the drawing was made? Perhaps a vision-questing journey inspired it. Maybe it symbolized good hunting. People's spiritual and physical lives then were wrapped up as one. The hunter believed an animal gave up its life for him, so that he could survive. The land had to provide, or he perished. We often carried tobacco on our trips. It was a traditional way of giving thanks and connecting with the land. Here, we left our gift of tobacco in remembrance of a time when beavers were the only ones that made dams.

Farther upstream on a portage trail, we watched a large black bear forage on sweet wild strawberries. We loved contemplating the lives of the animals we had the good fortune to meet along the way. Imagine being a female black bear and denning up for winter in a hollow tree, and giving birth to tiny, blind cubs so effortlessly that you don't actually wake up until some two months after their arrival. Imagine giving your little cubs the essential education in all the available foods: the berries, fish, insects, nuts, plants, and small mammals. What a different life it would be!

With the sun broadside and the wind to our backs, we paddled south from Rabbit Point. We watched our shadows on the rock walls beside us. Our arms swinging together in cadence with our torsos fused to the shape of the canoe that moved along swiftly beneath us. A flock of several dozen white gulls flew silently up off the Whale's Backs rocks. This was the place where we had fallen in love. This was the lake that we had crossed in a November ice storm fourteen years ago nearly sinking the canoe along with a trunkful of wedding gifts. This was where we had spent our first year living together and planning our first canoe expedition.

◄○►

We met up with old-growth forest scientists Peter Quinby and Tom Lee at their base camp for Ancient Forest Explorations and Research at the north end of Rabbit Lake in early July. Quinby's fieldwork, along with the research and education emerging from different associations such as the Wildlands League and World Wildlife Fund Canada, had all been drawing attention to the fact that old-growth red and white pine are an endangered species and should be preserved.

Plots ringed by flagging tape delineated their old-growth forest study areas. We spent part of the afternoon with a dozen international volunteers from five countries. Each person had been given a small site to identify all the plant matter and divide it up by percentage of species found. Particularly, they were identifying "indicator species" of plants that favour or need old-growth forest characteristics to survive. Whether plant, animal, or insect, the presence of indicator species assist in making a quick assessment as to the overall picture of a particular habitat. We know, for instance, that an undisturbed old-growth Great Lakes forest with a lot of ancient cedar will invariably be home to pine marten, a small member of the weasel family that hunts red squirrels.

Late in the afternoon, thunder rumbling in from the Ottawa Valley sent us hurrying back to our canoe. Deep purple clouds curling off towards the horizon like horizontal tornadoes threatened rain before nightfall, and we wanted to make camp.

Over the next few days, the weather became cooler, attracting mosquitoes that swarmed thickly after dark. By day, mayfly hatches were drawing the trout to the surface and the gulls from the air. Whole flocks of small white gulls swooped down deftly snatching the mayflies on the wing and off the water. Mayflies begin life underwater, then emerge along the lakeshore to metamorphose from nymph casings into fairy-like winged beauties. All in one day of our lives, the cycle of life for the mayfly completes itself as they take flight, find a mate, drop invisible eggs upon the water, then become dinner for another creature.

On the shores of Cassels Lake, connected to Rabbit and Snake lakes, we located the White Bear Forest Trails. We left the canoe at the trailhead and started up through a forest that immediately gave us that undeniable impression of wholeness. There is a harmonious feeling to an old-growth forest, where complex relationships exist between a seemingly endless variety of flowers, ferns, mosses, fungi, trees, insects, birds, and mammals. The slow decay of abundant dead wood, nursery logs, standing snags, and fallen branches provide a constant source of nutrients for the forest. This kind of healthy forest operates in perfect, self-sustaining harmony from the soil up to the forest canopy. We were pleased to see the map signposts recently erected by the town of Temagami to encourage both the locals and summer visitors to hike the trails and appreciate the beauty and diversity of an old-growth forest.

The portage out of the chain of lakes Rabbit, Cassels, and Snake and into Lake Temagami was situated beside the home of one of Temagami's long-time residents, Dorothy Zimmerman. A close family friend of Gary's, Aunt Dorothy was a warm and welcoming woman with a memory rich with the details of her adventurous life in Temagami. In 1932, she paddled in with her husband, Elly. Over the years, they built outpost cabins for rent, supplied ice blocks to summer residents, guided fishing trips, and raised a family of three. Many times she had related stories to us in her slow, careful way, each thought punctuated with soft laughter. Her house and family camp down the lake are filled with a lifetime of treasures, including shelves of painter's fungus etched with names, dates, and events, a journal of four generations. We stopped for tea and homemade cookies and to catch up on the latest news, in particular, about the restoration of the village train station. Before the highway, Dorothy could remember always meeting the trains. "I remember the train so well," she chuckles. "Everyone went to meet it at 8 p.m. no matter what. It was a place to visit, to see who was coming and going . . . to meet friends." Grey Owl arrived in Temiskaming by train in 1906, long before the advent of roads. Within a year he was living the life he had romanticized as a boy.

◄◦►

Our trip through the town of Temagami took us past the train station and the Busy Bee, where we sat outside enjoying Muffy's famous buttertarts and ice-cream cones before resupplying at the grocery store. Owners of one of the twelve hundred islands that freckle Lake Temagami's clear green waters plied us with an invitation to stay the night. The cottages on the islands tell a story of the generations of families that arrived first by train and steamboat and now by vehicle and motorboat. Our favourite cabins are those that face west, the small ones constructed of weathered grey logs tucked back in the forest. At sunset, their windows are glinting eyes, reflecting the brilliant hues of cerise, crimson, and orange.

As we paddled out of Obabika Inlet, Kalija jumped to her feet and began to growl. What looked like a floating log in the channel turned out to be a sleek, healthy-sized black bear. He emerged from the water and after a vigorous shake bounded up the scree slope, sending a small avalanche of rocks tumbling behind him. We watched the bear with eyes and ears, but Kalija employed a keen sense of smell as well. Kalija would often detect and alert us to the presence of wildlife long before we would have known through our own senses.

◄◦►

One enchanted morning as puffy cumulous clouds reflected off Obabika Lake's turquoise surface, Gary's long-time fishing companion was accidentally knocked overboard. I immediately dove into the water after the object as it spiralled downwards. I arrived back at the surface, breathless and dismayed. "Never mind," Gary said. "Offering my most prized possession, my special left-handed reel that I have had since I was six, surely has to bring us good luck." Just then, a low-flying blue heron swept past, guiding us up the lake.

Camping on a sandspit towards the north end of the lake, no doubt used by the Anishnabai for thousands of years, led to another happy coincidence. Alex Mathias, one of the local Anishnabai elders, arrived by boat from his cabin across the lake that evening. He had heard from other travellers that we were coming and he wanted to meet us. He carried a sheaf of old black-and-white photographs of himself as a boy and pictures of his family camped at this very place. Alex welcomed us as the head of the Misabai family, whose lands we now paddled through. He explained how his people had a different sense of ownership, how generations of his people had divided the land into family hunting grounds. He also explained the

Camping is a time to rest, watch the fading light, and listen to the sounds that you never noticed throughout the day.

responsibility of honouring the generations that had come before us and the necessity of respecting the rights of the generations that would follow us. Later, he donned a buckskin coat and feathered headdress and walked over to visit with a group of young canoeists camped nearby. Gathered there beneath the pines, with the campfire smoke wafting out through the trees, his appearance brought to mind images described by Grey Owl of native elders, even the image of Grey Owl himself, clad suitably Indian for his mainly British audience. Sixty years after Grey Owl's time, Alex's appearance still satisfied the long-held fantasy for these children of what it would be like to meet a "real Indian." Their fascination made them oblivious even to the annoying mosquitoes.

The following morning we were invited to a family breakfast at Alex's cabin. He made blueberry pancakes over an open fire burning beneath an old metal spring bed. We spent a full day with him, hiking the Obabika Trails at the north end of Obabika Lake. Ten kilometres (six miles) of trails meander through one of the world's largest concentrations of old-growth red and white pine. The Obabika Old Growth Forest, in the heart of what is known as the Wakimika Triangle, is an area of enormous spiritual and cultural significance to the Teme-Augami Anishnabai. Within the area, there is an old village site (Obabika Koo-jee-jing), two spiritual rocks (Kokomis and Shomis), a traditional winter fishery, prehistoric and historic archeological sites like cemeteries, culturally modified trees, agricultural plots and spiritual sites, dozens of pictographs, and the nastawgan, the old trails.

Hiking through the Obabika Old Growth Forest with Alex, our feet fell upon soft earth stitched together with the roots of many plants, flowering shrubs, mosses, lichens, ferns, and fungi. Goldthread, snowberry, and twinflowers formed

Temagami Anishnabai elder Alex Mathias stands beneath old-growth red and white pine known as the Three Sisters found along the Obabika old-growth trails.

a fine tapestry over the roots of the towering red and white pine, ancient spruce and cedar. There were snags, the dead standing trees full of pileated woodpecker holes, and fallen nursery logs that continue "living" through the seedling trees and mosses that take root along their decaying bark. On the shores of a narrow lake with a backdrop of precipitous cliffs, we rested for a while. Alex explained that this was Chee-skon-abikong Saw-gi-hay-gun-ning, meaning "the lake at the place of the huge rock." He pointed out the natural column of rock across the lake from us and told us it represented one of the most spiritually important sites to his family in all of Temagami. "This was the place I came with my father and my grandfather. This is where we always go to ask the Great Creator for guidance."

◄○►

The rain that swept across the face of Maple Mountain and down the length of Tupper Lake beating a furious tattoo drove away July's heat and humidity for a short spell. We had been forewarned of the changing weather the night before when, to the west and east, thunder rumbled through the billowing cumulous clouds of orange and purple streaked with bolts of lightning. As we paddled up to the base of Ontario's second highest peak, we could barely see the firetower on the summit. The rain ceased, and waves of mist rose in layers between the forested hills. It looked as if the mountain was blanketed with smouldering fires. The footing was boggy as we started up the trail and it began to get hot and humid. The path grew rockier and more steep until we reached the exposed summit dotted with thick carpets of flowering laurel and ripening blueberries. Two ravens greeted us as we admired the view, a three-dimensional map of interconnecting lakes. Staring off into the hazy

distance, we could almost trace the route we had covered since our journey's beginning thirty-five days ago.

Maple Mountain's native name, Chee-bay-jing, means "the place where the spirits go." It was once tribal tradition to lay bodies, after death, at the foot of the mountain. We were discovering such connections of people to the land everywhere along the nastawgan, the web of waterway routes and land trails that criss-cross the four-thousand-square-mile Temagami region. An intricate knowledge of the land evolved over some six thousand years to create the nastawgan. This web of routes navigating all kinds of terrain is unparalleled in size anywhere in North America. For thousands of years, the trails were used summer and winter. Bridges were even constructed for crossing creeks and gullies, and ramps and ladders were erected for scaling rock ledges.

◄○►

It was midsummer by the time we reached the western side of the Temagami region by paddling through the Lady Evelyn-Smoothwater wilderness. We passed through a congregation of twenty-five loons one afternoon. The gull chicks were all able to fly, and the flowers of bunchberry, mayflower, and blue-bead had turned to green berries. But best of all, the blueberries were ripening. We had our first good feast amongst their pollinators, the blackflies, on the top of Chee-bay-jing and every day since along the portage trails. The delicious berries reminded us of the good the pesky blackflies can do.

Scree slopes along the Lady Evelyn River were made up of pale-coloured rock as smooth as soapstone and as slippery as wet soap. The portages, strewn haphazardly with scree rock, forced us to move from boulder to boulder. In the bays upstream from the rapids, there were meadows of long grass, rushes, and cedar, perfect places to see moose. At Katherine Lake, low thunder rumbled all around us. We had set the canoe up between two trees to act as a roof for our shelter. The winds fanned out across the little lake, whipping it into a frenzy. Sheets of rain soon obliterated the forest and hills. Incredible cloud formations piled up like whipped cream over the forks of the Lady Evelyn. For another hour we crouched beneath the canoe. While waiting for the rain to stop, we studied the patterns of colour and texture on the wet bark of the largest red pine we had ever seen. Then, as sudden as the deluge of rain came, a burst of sun appeared and the white-throated sparrow heralded a rainbow with its "all's clear" song.

As seen from the canoe a kilometre away, the naked timbers bristling out from the hillside were like quills sticking out from the back of a porcupine. As we drew closer, our grim first impression of the effects of a fairly recent forest fire gave way to wonder. The forest floor was lush with the growth of blueberry bushes, fireweed, sarsaparilla, mosses, shrubs, and pine seedlings. The heat of fire had burned away the top layer of the forest floor, revealing mineral soils much favoured by conifers. Some, like Jack pine, actually require the heat of a forest fire to open their hard cones. The heat of fire also kills off harmful parasites, bacteria, and fungi, giving the ecosystem a fresh, new start. No creature wants to be caught in a forest fire, but the magic of the forest's rebirth makes the process complete and natural. Fire is not an enemy to the forest; clearcutting is. Vast clearcut land-scapes that grow across northern Ontario like a cancer are very different. Anyone who has flown over northern Ontario and seen examples of this barren landscape can attest to the brutal finality of the forest ecosystem under this destructive practice.

At Gamble Lake, we took the chance that we would make it to our campsite before the next storm. Then a bend in the river revealed the full fury of an angry cloud front marching straight down the Lady Evelyn River towards us. We were moving the paddles as fast as our shoulders and arms could rotate them. Angling the canoe towards shore, we landed and hurled everything into the long grass, flipped the canoe, and burrowed down just as the first big raindrops hit. An earsplitting crack of thunder made me jump. Kalija's eyes were wide with fear. Gary had one arm around each of us as we crouched in the shelter of our overturned canoe. Then the smell of smoke and charred wood wafted down. No doubt a Jack pine on the ridge above us had been shredded by that first bolt of lightning. It was the second time in as many days we had had to hide from such a storm. If it were not for the rain, the lightning could easily have started a forest fire.

Tracking upstream and portaging past lovely waterfalls on the Lady Evelyn eventually brought us to one of the headwater lakes for this river. It took more than 3 kilometres (2 miles) of portaging from Gamble to Sunnywater – the longest on the entire entire journey – and another half-day from there to Smoothwater and Apex lakes. Each lake was aptly named. This is an important area where streams, bogs, wetlands, and lakes flow through the surrounding forest, feeding three river systems: the Lady Evelyn, the Montreal, and the Sturgeon.

◄○►

Following the chain of lakes south to Mihell and Scarecrow Lake, we were surrounded by hillsides clothed in the richest, loveliest, most fantastic stands of white and red pine. From the shores of Scarecrow Lake, we could see the firetower on Ishpatina Ridge, Ontario's highest point of land. It took us an hour and a half to hike from Scarecrow Lake to the top of Ishpatina. We travelled along the lakeshore, through two bogs

On the portage trail through a relatively recent burn, rebirth, not destruction, is the recuring theme. Lady Evelyn River.

and past a gnarled old cedar and a huge pine half-cut through with a broad axe years ago. The view from the top was magnificent. Our little tent was just visible on the island campsite below. To the east, we could see Maple Mountain, where we had been a week before. To the west, there was the Sturgeon River valley, where we were headed next. We ate lunch, picked a hatful of blueberries, took some photographs, and hiked back down to the lake for a swim.

A huge log-jam in the middle of the meandering Sturgeon River stopped dead our easy float trip to Paul Lake. For an hour, we cut trail through a maze of tag alders taking us around the obstacle. Gary positioned the canoe on the riverbank at a forty-five-degree angle. We loaded it and placed Kalija in the bow. We shoved the canoe, but instead of a smooth descent out onto the river, I accidentally slipped under the hull, grabbing the gunwale and pulling the bow down. The whole canoe submarined into the river with Kalija still sitting in the bow submerged up to her neck. It was a difficult job to extricate all the sodden packs and the heavy communications case, get the canoe upright again and loaded. We were mud head to toe by the time we were done.

On Paul Lake, our rendezvous for a food package was perfectly timed. Having just completed the job of washing all the mud from our bodies and clothes, we heard the Beaver aircraft coming. We jumped in the canoe and paddled away from shore to meet the plane on the lake. Margaret Watson circled once and landed skilfully, taxiing right up to us as if she were driving a car. This small, strong, vivacious redheaded woman who owned and operated Sudbury Aviation was ready with laughter and generous with smiles. She had kindly brought in one of our prepackaged supply boxes. Knowing what travelling in the bush is like, she had also brought us in a loaf of fresh

bread, salad from her garden, fruit, and chocolate bars. Rather than portaging the extra weight, we opted to enjoy all the treats in one big binge that evening.

Unable to locate the original trail out of Paul Lake, we finally set off following the double track of an all-terrain vehicle trail that came down to the river's edge. For a few minutes the trail led us through the cool shadows of a Jack pine forest moist with sphagnum mosses and rustling with birch and ferns. Then we emerged onto a logging road, baked hard under the blazing sun. The only green things were hardy little poplar saplings thrusting their way into this dry, dusty world. It took us more than two hours to ferry our two loads to the first of a series of little height-of-land lakes between the Sturgeon and Wanapitei rivers.

Quite by chance, we met up with some canoeists from Algonquin Park's Taylor Statton Camp out on an all-summer adventure. Having just travelled the route between these lakes, they warned us of some hard slogging ahead through overgrown and boggy trails. Gary would lead with the canoe, weaving through the cedars, crawling over fallen logs, and squelching through knee-deep mud. He was good at finding the trails. Some of the fallen pine logs I scrambled over were waist-high. I straddled them without my feet touching the ground. The black spruce limbs were cat's claws scraping our forearms until they bled. We swatted and swore as the mosquitoes swarmed. Many times the vegetation was too thick even to see our feet, but we always managed to find the old trails impressed in the earth by travellers in times gone by. Our route took us from lake to small lake for three days.

At the brink of a wild whitewater chute on the Wanapitei River where I steadied the canoe, Gary stepped out onto a giant pine log, preparing to load the heavy communications case. Suddenly it rolled forward, causing him to fall back and very nearly impale himself on a rusty spike. The split-second trauma resulted in a bruised and swollen foot, but it was sobering to think what worse might have been. It took us a week to portage and paddle from the Sturgeon River, across the height of land lakes and up the Wanapitei River to its head-waters on Scotia Lake. The Wanapitei flowed steadily towards us. One afternoon we snaked through fields of grasses swaying so tall above our heads it was like being in a cornfield. We could see for a distance marsh hawks, a couple of eagles, and a pair of young black bears that Kalija smelled long before we reached them. They scurried for the nearest big pine and scrambled up the rough, fissured bark to a safe place on the tree's sturdy lower limbs. Ancient cedar overhung the river where the white water lilies bloomed in profusion, truly the beauties of the wetlands. And finally an old dam, a portage, and we were into Scotia Lake.

A warm reception awaited us at one of Marg Watson's tidy outpost cabins. She had flown in especially with fresh food and an invitation for a sauna. Our conversation turned to the importance of preserving what we have left of the roadless ancient forest in northern Ontario. Over the years, the number of remote fly-in camps that Marg operated had fallen to two-thirds as logging roads infiltrated everywhere, drawing in their wake the all-terrain vehicles that easily opened lake access legal or otherwise right down to the lakeshore. A mere 1 per cent of designated tourism lakes remain accessible only by portage and paddle or by seaplane. Grey Owl would not recognize some of the country that so deeply influenced his writing and public speaking. His words promoting the economic value of preserving wilderness, so poignant seventy years ago, could not be more truthful today.

◄○►

For a full day, we paddled upstream on one of our favourite northern Ontario whitewater rivers, the Spanish. The water level was low, and its colour was like clear brown tea. Small falcons called merlins dipped and dove along the cliffs where sweeping ridges of white pine still survived. At Sheahan (once called Wye), where the railway stopped along the Spanish River, we explored the grassy clearing with its handful of buildings that was once a thriving logging community of 250 families. We walked across the well-used portage between the Spanish River and Pogamasing Lake, and camped where a Hudson Bay out-post was once situated.

Travelling on the next morning, we first noticed tomb-stones overlooking the blue waters, nestled beneath red and Jack pine. Through binoculars I could read the family names of Plaunt and Mahaffy. One stone read "Here lies William Bell Plaunt In the woods & the waters he loved so well. Born Renfrew County 7th April 1879. Died Sudbury 23rd Oct 1960." A row of older cottages painted white with green trim were strung out along the bay beneath the pines. When six golden retrievers bounded down to the beach, Kalija could not contain her excitement. She leapt from the canoe and waded in to greet them. She loved cottages and porches, big friendly dogs and people. We were hailed ashore and treated to breakfast by the families who represented five generations of William Bell Plaunt's offspring. A tour of the cottages followed. One building was the cook shack, another place was where the ice house once stood. On rainy days, they told us, you could smell the horses in the place where the barn once stood. Black-and-white photographs described a family history reaching back to logging days in the Ottawa Valley. Small pine staked and cared for had been planted everywhere, and perhaps in ten more generations, they will be splendid reminders of the forests of giant trees that once connected Pogamasing Lake with the Ottawa Valley.

◄◦►

Surfing the canoe downwind through the whitecaps stirred by a strong northerly blow, we were carried onto a small beach and the beginning of another portage between the series of pretty lakes called Dennie, Gilden, Sinaminda, Landry, and Dusty. We noticed the fresh tracks of a timber wolf. Later at our campsite, just as I was writing up the weekly newspaper story, two bull moose swam from the mainland to our island. It was easy to imagine Grey Owl paddling on these quiet little lakes in connection with a natural landscape free of roads and human intervention.

As a bald eagle passed overhead, sun highlighted its white head and tail feathers. Great dark wings formed an unmistakable silhouette that we have come to recognize a kilometre away. An eagle's nest nearby was held securely between two lower limbs of an ancient white pine, a necessary platform for a structure that must have weighed close to a ton. A young eagle, all brown in colour and fully grown, beheld us from its perch above the nest in Buddha-like fashion. Later, a man in Biscotasing confirmed that he had seen them nesting here for more than sixty years, and in all likelihood the nest was established long before then.

In a week of travel, we had come another 150 kilometres (90 miles), zigzagging our way from Scotia Lake through Lake Onaping, downstream on Bannerman Creek and upstream on the Spanish, portaging between the small lakes, and then up through Mozhabong Lake to Biscotasing, a community at the crossroads of watersheds in four directions, and on to Ramsey Lake and the Mississagi River's headwaters. Grey Owl had paddled this way often in his life as a trapper, canoe guide, and "fire ranger."

◄◦►

We nosed the canoe into a swaying field of wild rice at the Spanish River headwaters, part of Mississagi River Provincial Park. The "wheat of the marshlands" was casting next year's crop of seed across the water. Some green husks were turning purple-brown, but most would not ripen until autumn. The native people's traditional harvesting method, still used today, consisted of paddling through the stalks and beating them with a stick to fill the canoe with rice. Spirits of people living here for thousands of years permeated our thoughts constantly. From the rice to the ripened berries, from the fish to the waterfowl to the moose and the bear, this area abounded with plant and animal life that had sustained a people who lived directly from the land. We watched loons with young feeding on schools of small perch. We marvelled as an osprey suddenly dropped out of the sky and plunged into the water, its body completely disappearing underwater as it struggled with its prey, then rising victorious, flapping off with a pickerel clutched firmly in its sharp talons.

At the end of one portage, we came to a wooden box on a stand that contained the Mississagi River Provincial Park sign-in book. We thumbed through the pages, finding names of several people we knew including a greeting for us from someone we had met in Temagami more than six weeks ago. Receiving this note so long after it was written reminded us of postal delivery two centuries ago when mail in this region was delivered by dogteam or canoe.

For most of a week, we paddled through Mississagi River Provincial Park, a waterway park that encompasses the Spanish

Campsite on the Mississagi River near Bark Lake.

River headwaters and the upper Mississagi River. There were headwater lakes, ponds, wetlands, and several bald eagle and osprey nests. We named one place where the forests were particularly thick with red and white pine "Avenue of the Pines." In a bay near the confluence of White Owl Lake and Mississagi Lake, Gary spotted a mother bear and her cub. In the grey, late-afternoon light with the wind offshore, we were fortunate to get so close. We floated nearby as the mother ambled past over stones and logs. The tiny black cub scrambled and whined, trying hard to keep up, but every rock was a mountain, every tree limb a major obstacle. Several kilometres later, we watched the antics of three otters diving for freshwater clams, which they brought to the surface to eat.

We could not have asked for a finer conclusion to the day than the Jackson family welcome. As we rounded the riverbend, a cabin came into view, and just like in a movie, the door flung open and children poured out. An older voice hailed us from amidst it all, "Won't you come in for cookies fresh from the oven?"

When the cookies and stories were done, we were invited to stay the night. Richard, our host and the most senior member of the Jackson clan, told us he was wondering how his expectant daughter was doing in Dayton, Ohio. Gary pulled out the satellite phone and said, "What's the number?" Fifteen more appreciative and happy faces could not be seen when Richard called out, "They've called her Tracy Lynn!"

The next day an east wind told us rain was on its way and we were glad. A long dry spell had turned the birch leaves yellow, shrivelled up the blueberries and bunchberries, and dried the mosses and lichens to crisp, fire tinder. By morning, we were packed just in time. A bag of toffees given to us by a friend was heartily enjoyed, one candy each kilometre. On Rocky Island Lake, the water level in the reservoir for the Mississagi River's Aubrey Falls dam was very low. So low that we were paddling through a graveyard of stumps usually hidden by the water. At the west end of Rocky Island Lake, we made two portages around the dams that harness the power of Aubrey Falls. The hydro-electric generating station reminded us of our free use of energy gathered from the sun over the summer. It was important to charge our battery to operate the communications equipment. Gary placed the solar panels in the sun at every opportunity. The green glow of the charging mechanism on the satellite phone would illuminate our tent throughout the night.

The Aubinadong River and its west branch to Megisan, Gord, and Lance lakes marked the last upstream leg of our journey to Lake Superior. A great grey owl on silent wings swooped out across the river and disappeared into a stand of older Jack pine. In many places, the only big trees of spruce, cedar, and pine remaining grow on steep cliffs or hang precariously close to the river's edge. As we walked upstream with the cool waters swirling around our ankles, our conversation was focused on the route ahead into the Algoma Highlands. The low level would make it extremely difficult, but we weren't ready to give up after months of planning and more than seventy days of paddling and portaging.

◄○►

At each new section of river, we had to decide how to proceed. We could either walk upstream pulling the canoe behind us (which was very slow), we could paddle through the shallows (which was quite exhausting because of all the strokes we have to take), or we could use a technique called "poling." We each found a poplar pole, debarked and smooth from a beaver's

Pushing the canoe over a beaver dam on the West Aubinadong River.

gnawing and the river's persistent flow. Standing in the canoe and taking a foot-forward stance, we used these poles, measuring a little less than half the length of our canoe, to enable us to travel much faster upstream. I avoided the rocks and judged the depth. Gary followed my lead. The crystal-clear waters revealed a river bottom of red, white, and black rocks, some round and some sharp, some slippery and some rough. I felt a bit like a kingfisher hovering and waiting for a meal.

Low water levels had left the West Aubinadong looking more like a black cobble laneway than a river. Staring dejectedly upstream, we conceded that it was time to portage despite the fact that a steady rain had soaked the lichen-covered rocks, creating footing as slippery as greased ballbearings. At day's end when a barred owl swooped across our path near a spit of sand and mud pockmarked with moose and timber wolf tracks, we decided it was time to camp. Between rain showers, we put up the tent and threw our belongings inside. Without thinking, I flung my sleeping bag up to Gary from the canoe like a football. It went straight up and over his head, bouncing off the tent roof and into the river. Launching myself off the bank, I grabbed it, realizing belatedly that I would be soaking the only dry clothes I had. We couldn't help but laugh as I stood firmly planted in ankle-deep mud. The day's progress had been only 4 kilometres (2.5 miles) in ten hours!

The Aubinadong had a way of luring us on. Just when the low water and rocks had us convinced to turn back, the channel deepened into a copper snake. Just when deadfalls made portaging the canoe impossible, the trail would improve. Finally, one evening under the colours of a rainbow and billowing clouds, we portaged into Torrence Lake. A mink, a loon with its lone chick, and a pair of ospreys greeted us. One more portage and we were into Megisan Lake.

Pulling the canoe and Kalija upstream in the shallow waters of the Aubinadong River.

Reaching this point was a highlight. This was the forest that we had discovered while exploring the Lake Superior watershed, and it was the inspiration for this journey. Everywhere we paddled and portaged from Megisan to Lance Lake, white pine seedlings were bursting forth. These waters form the headwaters to five watersheds that flow to Lake Huron, the Aubinadong-Mississagi, and Lake Superior via the Goulais, Batchawana, Chippewa, and Montreal rivers. Archeologists have uncovered evidence that aboriginal people used the area for a long time. Who knows how long it will remain untouched, but for the moment we were optimistic.

Tea-coloured waters flowed beneath huge overhanging cedars. Into deep, dark pools, we dropped worms on barbless hooks to entice the lively speckled trout. The marshes flourished with blackbirds and ducks. We paddled to within a canoe's length of a bittern that stood stock-still, pointing its beak straight up, camouflaging itself as a tall thin reed. On the small lakes, loons were beginning to gather in larger groups.

Part of the adventure of canoeing in this part of Algoma is that the trails are not like the well-groomed, yellow-signed ones found in the provincial parks. Black spruce and Jack pine are scarred with old blazes that ooze with white resin. The axe marks on poplars have turned grey. On one huge pine, we found a blaze in the shape of a man. According to a local trapper, it was carved by a family that lived on Gord Lake around 1910. In the trampled-down stripe of a path in the moss, we came across piles of bear and moose scat. These trails may have originally been animal paths between lakes that were later followed by aboriginal people travelling on foot and snowshoe.

◄○►

Pushing back the tangle of overhanging moose maples and stepping across a narrow channel in the forest floor, we got down on hands and knees to examine a tiny trickle of water. This was one of the rivulets feeding the headwaters of Farewell Creek. Our first thought was that we could not even float a balsam stick down this, let alone a canoe. We were barely able to figure out the direction of its flow in order to follow it to Flange Lake. A kilometre separated Lance Lake at the north end of the Aubinadong watershed with Flange Lake at the east end of the Montreal River watershed. We spent half a day from early dawn trying to establish a feasible trail between the two to avoid the black spruce bogs and the horrendous tangle of moose maples and balsam blowdowns. When a red-tailed hawk circled low and called out, we took it as a sign that the lake was near and struggled on. We arrived on the shores of tiny Flange Lake, encircled by mud flats that were dimpled with moose tracks. At the outlet, we found, to our enormous relief, a beaver dam and a span of river deep enough for our canoe. Dark tannin waters several inches deep flowed west over a sandy bottom. Farewell Creek was navigable after all. For us, it represented the 125th portage and the final questionable link in the waterway route between Algonquin and Lake Superior.

Farewell Creek and the Cow River wriggle through a boreal black spruce wetland quite unlike the West Aubinadong with its rocks and overhanging alders, cedars, and surrounding ridges of white pine. Below the final waterfalls on the Cow River, the Montreal is swallowed up by the reservoir lakes created by a series of dams from here to Lake Superior. There were places where the blond sand flats divided the Montreal into channels, and behind the dunes of silver driftwood, sandhill cranes congregated. A damp smell of old mud told us the water-level marks left in increments along shore were an additional

We arrived on Lake Superior by way of the westward-flowing Montreal River.

drop of 3 metres (10 feet) from spring water levels. This gave the rocky islands a funny appearance with their smooth grey skirts and top knots of trees.

In one day, we covered our greatest distance of the journey to date, 60 kilometres (40 miles) on mirror-calm waters that reflected scenery reminiscent of our travels up the Ottawa River two months ago. Sometimes we paddled way out in the middle where the sheer cliffs and their reflections divided by lake and sky became one. The silver path of our tiny canoe slicing the water formed a V similar to that made by beavers and loons as they swim across the surface.

Four dams harness the power created by this stretch of river falling more than 130 metres (430 feet) to Lake Superior. Back in the 1920s when Group of Seven artist J. E. H. MacDonald painted his canvas of autumn colours from the brink of Montreal Falls, I am sure he never thought of the painting as becoming an important historical record of this changed landscape. Despite the fact that it was only the end of August, birches and sugar maples were already beginning to set the forest aflame with brilliant yellows and reds. Hoisting up packs and canoe at the first dam, we made the portage just as the Agawa Canyon Tour Train passed through. Gary put Kalija on his shoulders and we waved back to the dozens of tourists gesturing with video cameras.

Our first view of Lake Superior was from the last headpond lake. It was a serene day and Montreal Island floated as a cloud in grey skies with only the horizon line anchoring it to earth.

Ecstatic with the deep clear water, we eagerly paddled out onto Lake Superior. As the first huge flock of southbound Canada geese passed high overhead, we felt the freshwater sea drawing us home like the end of a long migration.

THE HOME STRETCH

Under cloak of darkness, we stole out of Harmony Beach at 5:30 a.m., leaving behind the string of homes with friends who had so warmly greeted us the previous afternoon. After four days being windbound on Superior's shores, we were off to complete the last leg of our voyage to Fort St. Joseph.

Calm waters on Batchawana Bay reflected starlight, as if we were paddling through the universe. Soon an orchestra of light and sound choreographed by the rising sun began with a gentle swell. Pink mackerel skies followed as the North and South Sandy Islands were suddenly highlighted by the golden rays of morning. Wind crescendoed and waves crested, unnerving us once again, but we made it across Goulais Bay and around the orange-lichen-encrusted headlands of Gros Cap. People who had heard of us and our trip waved from their canoes and porches. By the time we had reached the historic Sault Canal, night was upon Sault Ste. Marie. City lights glimmered on the St. Mary's River, a waterway that has seen the passing of canoes for thousands of years. Our main concern in the darkness was not colliding with logs or rocks but rather a steel rod or cement pier. Downstream from the locks, our long day came to a close at a friend's home. In our flashlight beam, we read a freshly painted sign at the water's edge, "Welcome Home Joanie, Gary and Kalija!"

The shallow waters of Lake George on the St. Mary's River were milky with sediment. East winds persisted all night, stirring huge swells on Lake Huron. Our decision the following day to take the east side of St. Joseph's Island resulted in a thirty-two-kilometre detour when we paddled to Canoe Point and discovered we would have to take the shipping channel on the less windy west side of the island instead.

The wind forced us into the marsh grass, so tall we had to keep standing up in the canoe to see where we were going. In Haye Marsh, Gary caught sight of a paddle waving to us from shore. All our hard-earned kilometres that day ended with a surprise, a journey's end feast prepared by a friend who had somehow figured this was the spot where we would come ashore for our last night on the trail.

I awoke long before dawn and walked down to the shore. A misty rain was falling and the wind had died. I looked out on the wide expanse of river, the international boundary between Canada and the United States, and it brought to mind the strange nature of political and human ownership boundaries on the land and water. We had crossed them all summer, but they meant nothing to the hawks that migrate south every fall, the moose or the bear that must raise their young, find food, shelter, and a mate across a particular landscape. These boundaries mean nothing when you take a breath or a drink of water. We are all of one, and what influences one being ultimately affects the others. I began recalling campsites along the way. Each person we had met was like a long-time friend connected to the landscape we had paddled through.

Morning came early with the arrival of twenty-two other paddlers. Sixteen of them were dressed in voyageur costumes and ready to paddle three 36-foot voyageur canoes. Staff at the historic site of Fort St. Joseph had been following our progress and had planned this amazing celebration. As Gary left an offering of a braid of tobacco on the point, he asked for safe passage for our little entourage en route to the fort. As we made the "voyageur crossing," spirits could not be dampened by the rain. At the fort, one of the staff members had been up late the night before arranging the historical encampment and preparing the pea soup and bannock over an open fire.

Portaging around one of the Lady Evelyn River waterfalls.

I was at a loss for words. Someone handed me copies of the Saturday newspaper features and a printout of our Web site. I suddenly realized how much we had touched people's lives. They had been following this journey for more than ninety days. Besides the newspapers and the Web site, there had also been the weekly CBC Radio broadcasts. Thousands of readers and listeners had travelled with us across northern Ontario for the summer and I didn't need to try and summarize the experience.

—<o>—

In the months that followed the journey's conclusion, we hurled ourselves into the tug-of-war over whether the government would favour short-term industrial interests or long-term change in the way we treat all of nature. A thirteen-part television series filmed over the course of our journey went to air. We gave countless slideshow presentations to help people understand what was really at stake. This was the last chance to save some of these remaining ancient forests and all the biodiversity they harboured. The Partnership was hard at work educating the public and lobbying the government. Letters strongly supporting the preservation of our ancient forests and the old-growth pine poured into the premier's office. In the spring of 1999, the government made the momentous announcement that the province's system of protected areas would double in size with the addition of 378 new parks and protected areas. Many of the significant sites we had paddled through, including the old-growth Great Lakes forest of the Algoma Highlands and the ancient pine forests of the lower Spanish watershed, were going to be part of the system. New river parks would provide essential corridors between these sites. And importantly, an accord was drawn up with the Partnership and the forest industry to address the issues of biodiversity and the requirements of all wildlife on the managed lands.

Living for a while at the speed of nature, as we do on a long journey, makes us more aware of the world around us. When we smell, taste, touch, hear, and feel the world as intimately as children, our role becomes more than that of onlooker. Our sense of the realities of all living creatures is both astounding and humbling. If every ant were to leave Earth today, our own species would be doomed. If our species left the Earth today, the rest of creation would heave a sigh of relief. We must use our ability to imagine ourselves under the skin of a cougar, or in the seed of a pine, or in a drop of water travelling from ocean to sky and through the bodies of all living matter, because we are all of these things, all of the time.

THE JOURNEY IN PICTURES

Water flowing through the forest connects one river to another, to the ocean and the clouds and the bodies of all living things.

"At the foot I could plainly see, drawn up on the gravelly beach, the canoe brigade of my fellow-travellers, and for a long time I watched the river, there below me, racing madly on, singing, shouting in glee, rushing onward all unconscious of what lay before it, to its doom, onward to that grave of all lost rivers, the Ocean – fresh and furious in the Spring-time, tired and lazy in the Autumn, going on for ever, ever down to eventual oblivion.

"And I wondered, once it got there and realised it never could come back, did it sometimes have a longing for the mountains, or did it ever miss the trees, or be lonesome for the joyous, carefree days it had spent in the far-off Silent Places."

– TALES OF AN EMPTY CABIN, p. 158

The white flowers of bunchberries are a common sight along the portage trails in the early summer of the Great Lakes-St. Lawrence woodlands.

Cow moose with twin calves feeding on aquatic vegetation. Catfish Lake, Algonquin Provincial Park.

"As we approach the head of the River, the lakes become smaller and, because you can see most of every part of them at a glance, seem to be sort of intimate and friendly. In such places we occasionally see moose, huge beasts, upwards of six feet at the shoulder, who stand and stare at us curiously as we pass, perhaps the first humans they have ever seen. Mostly they are in the shallows near the shore, digging up water-lily roots, and often having their heads completely submerged, presently come up for air with a mighty splurge, and seeing us, stand a moment to watch, the water pouring in small cataracts from the pans of their wide antlers. Invariably deciding that we are not to be trusted, they spin on their heels with surprising agility for so large an animal and lurch away at a springy, pacing trot that is a deal faster than it looks; and the noise of their going, once they hit the bush, is something like that of a locomotive running loose in the underbrush."

– *TALES OF AN EMPTY CABIN, p. 204*

Trout lily. Algonquin Provincial Park.

We awaken in our tent to the sound of flowing water beckoning us onwards.

A misty spray hangs over the Amable du Fond River.

Twinflowers, along with gold thread, creeping snowberry, trailing arbutus, bearberry, and wintergreen weave the forest soils into a mat of surface life.

"Here, even in these modern days, lies a land of Romance, gripping the imagination with its immensity, its boundless possibilities and its magic of untried adventure. Thus it has lain since the world was young, enveloped in a mystery beyond understanding, and immersed in silence, absolute, unbroken, and all-embracing; a silence intensified rather than relieved by the muted whisperings of occasional light forest airs in the tree-tops far overhead."

– THE MEN OF THE LAST FRONTIER, p. 30

Small chanterelles growing in the moist sphagnum moss on the floor of the old-growth forest.

A cool and foggy morning. Ottertail Creek in the Ottawa Valley.

In the Ottawa Valley, the forest canopy of old-growth white pine towers above the white spruce.

Bell-shaped yellow flowers precede the balloon-like poisonous berries of the blue-bead lily.

"And the joy of the Spring is in the sound of running water and the smell of new-blown flowers; it comes in the resounding, military tattoo of a woodpecker on a dry limb, the measured, muffled drumming of a ruffled grouse, in the sound of countless song-birds at the time of Dawn, in the shrill chattering of gulls wheeling whitely overhead, and the weird and wailing, half-human laughter of the loons. Something, too, of the freedom and the wanderlust of Springtime, surges through the blood of one who watches the spectacle of the migration of the geese, the flying phalanxes and legions of the wild-geese honking their way in broad V's and long, wavering lines towards the North – often a mile above the earth, yet the rushing beat of the mighty pinions is plainly audible."

– *TALES OF AN EMPTY CABIN*, p. 251

The berries on this widespread little dogwood herb, bunchberry, provide a favourite food for grouse and white-tailed deer.

White birch is a highly valuable tree as a medicinal and food source for many songbirds and mammals, including humans. Matabitchuan River.

To aboriginal people, the bark beneath the outer birch paper was useful in making baskets, dishes, wigwams, and canoes. Rabbit Lake.

A pair of entwined garter snakes soak the sun's warmth into their cold-blooded bodies. Snake Lake.

The lightweight, decay-resistant wood of the eastern white cedar is ideal for making canoes, cradleboards (tikinagan), wigwams, brooms, and rope.

Indian pipe growing in sphagnum moss is nourished through fungal connections from its roots to those of nearby trees.

We can't even begin to name all the species within a healthy ancient forest, let alone understand their complex relationships.

Obabika Inlet forms the northwest arm of Lake Temagami. A portage at its western end leads to Obabika Lake.

"And the brigade seems to move in a world of phantasma and unreality, as though the River were some strange, unearthly highway in another world where tall, dark beings, shrouded and without faces, gaze featurelessly from the river-banks upon us and stare and stare, or loom over us with ghostly whispering while some, to all appearance, beckon with impish, claw-like hands to stay us, with a hideous suggestion of blind-men reaching for us in the dark; while behind them lies a vast Kingdom of Gloom of which they are the dark inhabitants, and in whose shadowy thoroughfares untoward events lie crowded, imminently, ready to happen."

– TALES OF AN EMPTY CABIN, p. 217

Early morning from the top of Maple Mountain, or Chee-bay-jing, "the place where the spirits go," as it is known to the Teme-Augami Anishnabai.

Awakening to a chorus of songbirds and a mist-shrouded sunrise is a peaceful beginning to a day on the trail in Temagami.

"I sit alone. And all the Voices of the Night are all around me, and swift rustlings, soft whisperings and almost noiseless noises encompass me about.

"And the moon throws eerie shadows down along the aisles between the trees, where strange shapes and formless objects stand like waiting apparitions, where moonbeams lie in glimmering pools, and spots of light like eyes peer out from darksome ambuscade.

"On the shore, in a little group, some tiny beavers sit, and sniff, and look, and whisper low, like children seeing goblins in a graveyard."

– *TALES OF AN EMPTY CABIN, p. 334*

This twisted, little Jack pine, whose growth is stunted by weathering and a thin soil base, appears like an artistically pruned Japanese bonsai tree.

Wetlands, marshes,
bogs, and fens
are an essential
part of the ancient
forest landscape.
Lake Temagami.

"Human beings, as a whole, deny to animals any credit for the power of thought, preferring not to hear about it and ascribing everything they do to instinct. Yet most species of animals can reason, and all men have instinct. Man is the highest of living creatures, but it does not follow as a corollary that Nature belongs to him, as he so fondly imagines. He belongs to it. That he should take his share of the gifts she has so bountifully provided for her children, is only right and proper; but he cannot reasonably deny the other creatures a certain portion. They have to live too."

– *TALES OF AN EMPTY CABIN, pp. 325-26*

Plentiful populations of amphibians are an excellent sign that the water and air are healthy.

The pattern of dry and wet rock reveals the profile of a face. Lady Evelyn River.

The Lady Evelyn River is part of North America's greatest prehistoric system of interconnected trails and water routes.

Chee-skon-abikong Saw-gi-hay-gun-ning ("the lake at the place of the huge rock") is one of the most spiritually important places in Temagami.

"In the wider spaces between the smooth grey hardwoods, stood the bodies of huge white pine, fluted red-brown columns upwards of six feet across, rearing their bulk up through the roof of leaves, to be shut off completely from further view; yet raising their gigantic proportions another half a hundred feet above the sea of forest, to the great plumed heads that bowed to the eastward each and every one, as though each morning they would salute the rising sun."

– *THE MEN OF THE LAST FRONTIER, pp. 131-32*

These towering white pine growing within the Wakimika Triangle are among the rarest great giants that remain on the Ontario landscape today.

*The Conjuring Rock at
the vision-questing site on
Chee-skon-abikong is a
spiritual focal point for the
Teme-Augami Anishnabai.*

This view of Centre Falls on the Lady Evelyn River has been admired by travellers for thousands of years.

The 3.5-kilometre (2.2-mile) portage into Sunnywater Lake from Gamble Lake was the longest carry on the entire journey.

"The town of Bisco was dropping fast astern as I dipped and swung my paddle, driving my light, fast canoe steadily Northward to the Height of Land. It was not much of a town as towns go. It had no sidewalks, and no roads, and consisted mainly of a Hudson's Bay store, a saw mill, probably fiftly houses scattered on a rocky hillside, and an Indian encampment in a sheltered bay of Biscotasing Lake, on the shores of which this village stood. But it was rather a noted little place, as, being situated within measurable distance of the headwaters of a number of turbulent rivers . . . and being moreover the gateway to a maze of water routes that stretch Southward to lakes Huron and Superior, and Northward to the Arctic ocean, the fame of its canoemen was widely known."

– PILGRIMS OF THE WILD, p. 8

A calm evening on Smoothwater Lake. Lady Evelyn-Smoothwater Provincial Park.

At the time the seeds for these trees germinated, the earliest European explorers were venturing westwards to the Upper Great Lakes.

Emulating the ecology of a naturally evolving forest is the challenge in a "managed" landscape.

Picking and eating wild blueberries is a highlight of a summer canoe trip. Biscotasing Lake.

"River, sublime in your arrogance, strong with the might of the Wilderness, even yet must you be haunted by wraiths that bend and sway to the rhythm of the paddles, and strain under phantom loads, who still thread their soundless ways through the shadowy naves of the pine forests, and in swift ghost-canoes sweep down the swirling white water in a mad *chasse galerie* with whoops and yells that are heard by no human ear.

"Almost I can glimpse these flitting shades, and on the portages can almost hear, faintly, the lisping rustle of forgotten footsteps, coming back to me like whispers from a dream that is no longer remembered, but cannot die."

– *TALES OF AN EMPTY CABIN, p. 166*

Bannerman Creek reflects the colours of forest and sky.

Fireweed appears in abundance after forest fires.

"From the tops of the birches on the hillsides there came a low whispering, a sound of rustling that never seemed to cease, as the wind played amongst the leaves, so that the Indians had named these highlands the Hills of the Whispering Leaves. The river banks were lined by a forest of tall, dark pine trees, and their huge limbs hung out over the water, far above it; and along the shore beneath them robins, blackbirds and canaries flew and fluttered, searching for their breakfast among the new grasses and the budding leaves of the pussy-willows. The air was heavy with the sweet smell of sage and wild roses, and here and there a humming-bird shot like a brilliant purple arrow from one blossom to another. For this was in May, called by the Indians the Month of Flowers."

– THE ADVENTURES OF SAJO AND HER BEAVER PEOPLE, p. 14

Pitcher plants are a carnivorous perennial, attracting and trapping insects in their deep, vessel-shaped leaves. Dusty Lake.

Dwarfed by the tall,
straight trunks of
old-growth red and
white pine near
Obabika Lake.

"Came a sound, a murmuring from the distance, a wind that stirred the tree-tops overhead; the sleeping forest half-awakened, sighed, and as the sound passed onward, slept again. And all around the golden and red leaves of the birch and maples, the spots of sunlight on the forest floor; and the thin blue wisp of smoke trailing up and up from the dying fire, up through the leaves and on beyond them. And far overhead the Unseen Musician improvised a low rambling melody in the many-stringed lyre of the pine-tops, and its soft humming, and the quiet lap, lap of the wavelets on the sandy shore, mingled with the old man's voice as he intoned in soft gutturals, with all the imagery to which his language lends itself."

– *THE MEN OF THE LAST FRONTIER, p. 244*

A view from the top of Ontario's highest point of land, Ishpatina Ridge. From the summit, there's a view in all directions.

This sandspit is one of more than a dozen significant archeological sites to be found on Obabika Lake.

"The River's shores are lined with forests that stretch back without interruption, save for their innumerable waterways, a hundred miles and more to the Eastward, and Westward clear to the shores of Lake Superior. There is every variety of timber common to that zone, and an ever-changing panorama unfolds itself along the River's course; the poplar woods, with their bright trunks, restless fluttering leaves and lightly shifting shadows; the tangled brakes of willows, ash or alders; the hard metallic green of birch and maple; rich, grassy meadows and purple fen-lands; the cloistered, brooding calm of towering pines; each kind takes its turn and passes in review on either bank."

– *TALES OF AN EMPTY CABIN, p. 165*

Dawn, a lone sandpiper, and the song of the winter wren made us feel fortunate to be there to appreciate it all. Marina Lake.

For the Iroquois and Seneca, the white pine symbolized a link between nations of people, as well as the heavens and earth. Scarecrow Lake.

Arriving at Haentschel Lake was the reward for numerous swampy, buggy, overgrown portages.

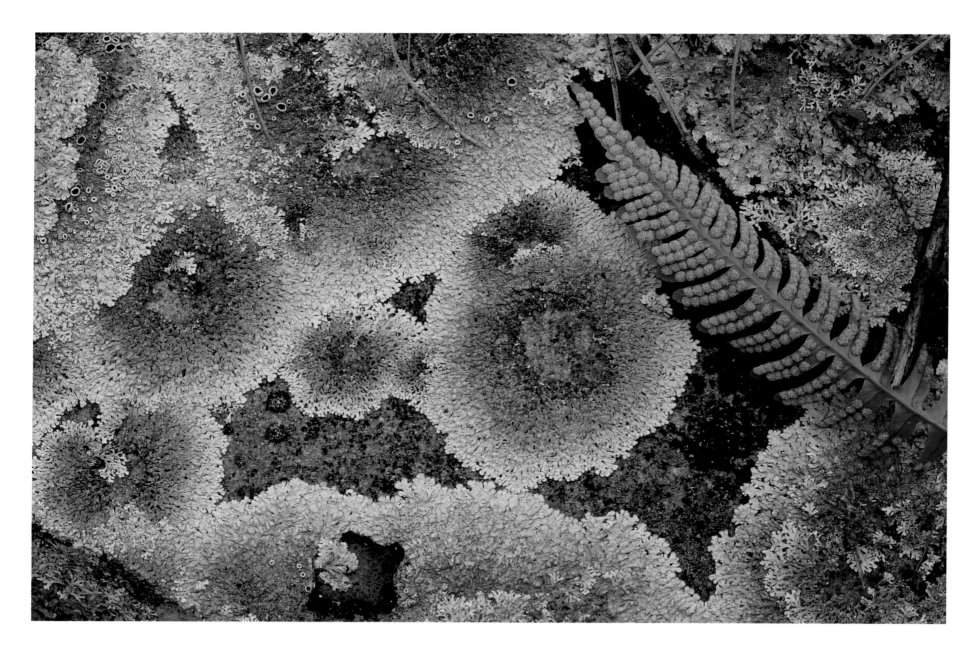

Map lichen and a fertile fern frond laying on the Canadian Shield granite rock.

"Behind me was an enchanted world of twilight forest, where the portentous silence was broken by no sound, save the occasional drip of dew from the leaves. On its floor one would have moved in a kind of pale translucence, as in some dim ocean cavern, where common objects loomed crouching, indistinct and shapeless, and the fronds of scattered clumps of undergrowth hung like queer aquatic-looking plants, in this green and liquid pool of murky light."

– *TALES OF AN EMPTY CABIN, p. 301*

Moss on a nursery log. The slow decay of abundant dead wood is an essential process to perpetuate the ancient forest landscape.

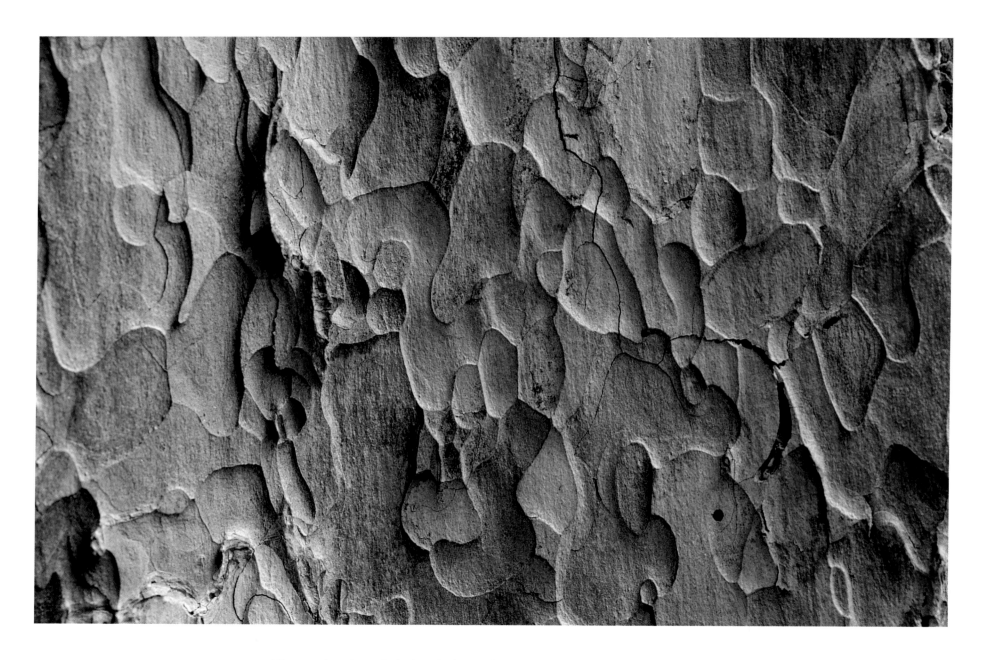

The inner layer beneath the heavily fissured bark of the white pine tree. Mississagi Lake.

Eastern white pine can live five hundred years, and attain a height of 50 metres (150 feet). Upper Bark Lake.

An essential ingredient in a healthy forest is the presence of trees that range widely in size and age. On the trail to Ishpatina Ridge.

"The distant mutter of the rapids, as we draw on it, swiftly becomes a growl, grows louder, and increases in volume by the minute, moving swiftly towards us, rising in diatonic progression up the scale of sound until it becomes a thunderous uproar. A hundred yards ahead the River suddenly drops abruptly out of sight, breaking off in a black, horizontal line from which white manes and spouts of foaming water leap up from time to time; below that – nothing, apparently, and the tree-lined banks fall away at what, from that distance, looks to be a most alarming angle. But now we feel the tug and pull of the tow. No more talk."

– *TALES OF AN EMPTY CABIN, p. 219*

We paddled upstream for three days on the twisting Wanapitei River.

Earth tongue mushrooms growing at the base of an eastern white cedar tree.

*Generations of travellers
have passed beneath this
ancient cedar, a matriarch
of the Great Lakes Forest.*

A campsite on Haentschel Lake afforded us a view to both the sunrise and sunset. The deep water next to the shoreline rocks was perfect for swimming.

"Not all the wild lands gloom in sullen shadow. There are vistas, unbelievably beautiful, to be seen beyond the boles of giant trees edging some declivity, of sun-drenched valleys, or wide expanse of plain, blue with its luscious carpet of berries. Occasional grassy glades, oases in the sameness of the sunless grottos surrounding them, refresh the mind and eye, seeming intimate and friendly after the aloofness of the stately forest."

— *THE MEN OF THE LAST FRONTIER*, p. 33

Reflection on the Sturgeon River.

A spiderweb draped over a small gilled mushroom. Old-growth pine forests are among the most productive places for mushroom growth.

Gilled mushrooms and coral lichen. Harvesting edible wild mushrooms is a lucrative industry, and another reason to preserve the ancient forests.

With its deep, blue waters, rocky outcroppings, and sandy coves, Scotia Lake reminded us of a miniature Lake Superior.

"In places vast mountainous upheavals of granite and Keewaydin stand high above the River, and on the face of them lone dwarfed and twisted trees cling precariously to ledges. There are sheer escarpments with queer images chiselled on them by the rain and frost of centuries, and sardonically featured gargoyles carved in stone, some sitting, others standing, others leaning outward from their eyries, all graven there immovably, looking forever down upon the hurrying, ceaseless procession of the River. And at length, as though wearied with the unending spectacle, the moun- tain turns about abruptly and bears off into the interior, standing like a forbidding, massive rampart, far into the distance; and at its flank deep, mysterious gullies lead back to undiscovered territories, ravines into which no ray of sunlight ever penetrated, and in which no human foot has ever trod."

– *TALES OF AN EMPTY CABIN, p. 165*

Artists and shamans of long ago used this rock wall as a canvas.

When Aubrey Falls was dammed, the forest surrounding the Mississagi River upstream was cut and flooded to create Rocky Island Lake reservoir.

Portaging over the bridge that spans the top of Aubrey Falls on the Mississagi River. Aubrey Falls Provincial Park.

*Aubrey Falls on the
Mississagi River.*

"Here and there along its course are mighty waterfalls, some with rainbows at the foot of them; and one of these thunders down a deep chasm, down two hundred feet into a dark swirling eddy, seemingly bottomless, that heaves and boils below the beetling overhang as though some unimaginably monstrous creature moved beneath its surface. And in the vortex of this boiling cauldron there stands a pinnacle of rock on which no creature ever stood, crowned with a single tree, forever wet with the rainbow-tinted spray that in a mist hangs over it, while the echoing, red walls of the gorge and the crest of the looming pines that overtop them, and the all-surrounding amphitheatre of the hills, throw back and forth in thunderous repetition the awe-inspiring reverberations of the mighty cataract. And as we stand and watch it, it is borne home to us what a really little figure a man cuts in this great Wilderness."

– *TALES OF AN EMPTY CABIN, p. 214*

Joanie pulling the canoe upstream on the Spanish River.

The sun is our life source, as is the water, air, and soil. Upper Bark Lake.

Canoeing beneath the cliffs at the south end of Mohzabong Lake en route north to Biscotasing.

*Sunset reflected
in a small pool
on the West
Aubinadong River.*

"Above my head, somewhere in the jack-pine, a white-throat commenced his carolling. The first few plaintive notes stole out into the silence tentatively, as though seeking a response, and, being answered, broke forth courageously into a full volume of song. Ever increasing in numbers, the feathered choir joined in the litany of joy and praise for the gift of a new day, until all around the air seemed full of harmony."

– *TALES OF AN EMPTY CABIN, p. 301*

Mist rising through pines on the Mississagi River.

Near the confluence
of the Mississagi
and Aubinadong
rivers, we surprised
a pair of playful
otters descending
the sandbank on
their bellies.

It is rare to see a canopy of white pine extending ridge to ridge as far as the eye can see.

Thoreau compared an unclouded sky to a meadow without flowers and a sea without sails. Megisan Lake, Algoma Highlands.

"Steadily, day after day, he had forged ahead, sometimes moving along easily on smooth water as he was now doing, at other times poling up rough rapids, forcing his frail canoe up the rushing, foaming water and between jagged, dangerous rocks with a skill that few white men and not all Indians learn. This morning his way was barred by a water-fall, wild and beautiful, higher than the tallest pine trees, where the sun made a rainbow in the dashing white spray at the foot of it. . . . Picking up the canoe, he carried it, upside down on his shoulders, over a dim portage trail between the giant whispering trees, a trail hundreds of years old, and on which the sun never shone, so shaded was it. He made a second trip with his light outfit, loaded his canoe, and out in the brightness and the calm water above the falls continued his journey."

– *THE ADVENTURES OF SAJO AND HER BEAVER PEOPLE, p. 15*

A forest "on fire" with the light of sunset. Becor Lake.

At the end of the eighteenth century, these ancient trees were the merest fraction of the forests that had spanned the Maritimes to the Mississippi.

On the West Aubinadong when the water was no longer deep enough for the canoe, we either walked up the riverbed or along the old, overgrown portages.

This small waterfall and stream in the Algoma Highlands are part of the top-of-the-watershed system of rivers that feed the mighty Mississagi River.

"Travelling in an unpeopled wilderness calls for an intense concentration on the trail behind, a due regard for the country ahead and a memory that recalls every turn made, and that can recognize a ridge, gulley, or stream crossed previously and at another place. Swinging off the route to avoid swamps, and other deviations must be accomplished without losing sight of the one general direction, meanwhile the trail unrolls behind like a ball of yarn, one end of which is at the camp and the other in your hand."

— *THE MEN OF THE LAST FRONTIER, p. 116*

Dewdrops on white pine needles.

When this tree was still standing, a pileated woodpecker hammered out a cavity that serves now as a dish to hold porcupine droppings. Megisan Lake.

"Above, below, and on all sides is moss; moss in a carpet, deadening the footfall of the traveller, giving beneath his step, and baffling by its very lack of opposition his efforts to progress. Moss stands in waist-high hummocks, around which detours must be made. Moss in festoons hangs from the dead lower limbs of the trees, like the hangings in some ancient and deserted temple. And a temple it is, raised to the god of silence, of a stillness that so dominates the consciousness that the wanderer who threads its deserted naves treads warily, lest he break unnecessarily a hush that has held sway since time began."

– *THE MEN OF THE LAST FRONTIER, pp. 32-33*

Moss is the forest's sponge that holds the moisture, slowly releasing it over time.

An ancient forest is quickly apparent by the wealth of biological diversity from the forest floor to the forest canopy.

At the north end of Lance Lake, boreal forest mingles with the northern range of the Great Lakes-St. Lawrence Forest.

Cirrocumulous are among the highest of clouds found at the height that jets fly. These mackerel, or fish-scale, clouds foretell of changing weather.

"These large lakes on the Northern watershed are shallow for the most part, and on that account dangerous to navigate. But in spots are deep holes, places where cliffs hundreds of feet high run sheer down to the water's edge, and on to unfathomed depths below. Riven from the lofty crags by the frosts of centuries, fallen rocks, some of them of stupendous size, lie on some submerged ledge like piles of broken masonry, faintly visible in the clear water, far below. And from out the dark fissures and shadowy caverns among them, slide long, grey, monstrous forms; for here is the home of the great lake trout of the region, taken sometimes as high as forty pounds in weight."

– *THE MEN OF THE LAST FRONTIER*, p. 31

Sunset on Lance Lake. Algoma Highlands.

Pouch-like clouds hanging beneath storm clouds mean heavy rain is near.

Our journey through the ancient forest by water represented for us the connectedness of all life across one land base.

Sunset on Lake Superior, the largest expanse of freshwater on Earth. North of Alona Bay.

"The great sun rises, goes on up, getting smaller but hotter as it goes, and becomes a burning red ball that beats down on unprotected heads and hands and faces. As the day advances the air becomes more torrid; the lakes lie vitreous, like seas of molten glass, and the palpitating landscape is immersed in a screeching, scorching glare. High overhead in a metallic sky the sun, like a burnished copper gong, beats a fierce tattoo to which the whole face of Nature quivers, and to whose tune the rows of jack-pines topping the distant ridges writhe, and swing, and sway in the steps of a fantastic sun-dance, reeling drunkenly in the shimmering waves of a merciless, breathless heat."

– *TALES OF AN EMPTY CABIN, p. 182*

Because they are so high above the earth, cirrus clouds hold the sunset's colour a long time after the sun drops below the horizon.

A brief period of splendid colour before a nightly view of star-speckled heavens. Mamainse Harbour.

"And the River has its moods, like any living thing, and no one stretch of it is like to any other. In some of its reaches a dark sullen flood, powerful and deep, flowing swiftly and smoothly with a high, forbidding precipice on either side, running the grim gauntlet of the mountain, on emerging will spring to sudden fury and become a raging, irresistible torrent, tearing madly at the banks that hem it in, to break quite suddenly into a rabble of chattering wavelets, clattering amongst the gravel of a shallows. Often it runs docilely along, carefree and singing, or murmuring and sleepy, more and more placid as it goes, until its current is quite gone and it broadens peacefully out into tranquil, island-studded lakes with deep bays and inlets and picturesque, bold rocky promontories, all black with pine."

– *TALES OF AN EMPTY CABIN, pp. 163-164*

Water flowing over rock.

Looking up through the layers of red and yellow sugar maple leaves.

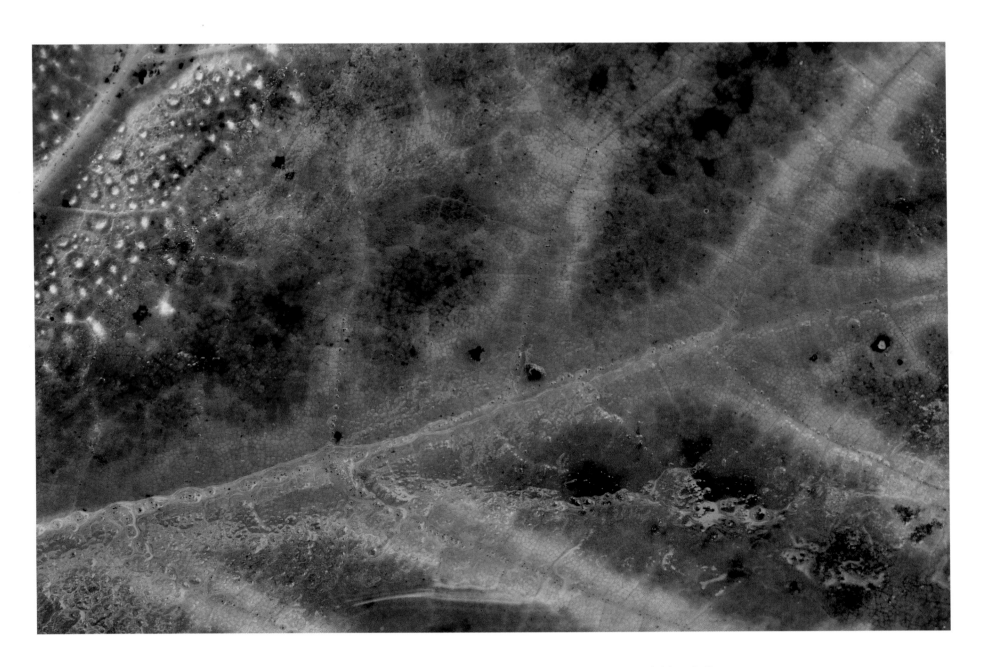

The colours of leaves change when shorter, colder days halt the production of chlorophyll.

Red pine bark.

Reflections on the Montreal River suddenly became a totem pole when we viewed the shoreline with our heads on one side.

In the latter part of Grey Owl's life, he became an ardent conservationist and protector of the endangered beaver. Beaver-cut, Algoma Highlands.

"The woods are full of crisp rustlings, as small beasts scamper over frosted, crackling leaves, intent on the completion of self-appointed tasks. The surface of the waters is broken by clusters of ducks and waterfowl of all kinds, noisily congregated for the fall migration. Along the shore-line, ever-widening V's forge silently ahead, as beaver and muskrats, alert, ready to sink soundlessly out of sight on the least alarm, conduct their various operations. Porcupines amble along trustfully in the open, regardless of danger; and, partly owing to their bristling armour and greatly owing to the luck of fools, generally escape unscathed. Back in the hills any number of bears are breaking off boughs and shredding birch-bark, to line dens that a man could be well satisfied to sleep in."

– *THE MEN OF THE LAST FRONTIER, p. 133*

White water lilies.

Our long journey spanned the seasons from spring to autumn. Gord Lake, Algoma Highlands.

Sugar maple trees of the Great Lakes-St. Lawrence Forest turn the forest yellow and red in autumn.

Lake Superior's colourful, wave-tumbled, perfectly smooth rocks.

We hope the Ancient Forest Water Trail will create awareness of the rarity of our ancient forests and the importance of preserving wilderness corridors.

ACKNOWLEDGEMENTS

To find out about and become involved in the protection of Ontario's wild spaces, contact the Partnership for Public Lands, <www.wildontario.org>. We are exceedingly grateful to the tireless efforts of many unsung heroes in organizations like these, and the foundations and individuals that fund their work. Special thanks to the Federation of Ontario Naturalists, <www.ontarionature.org>, the Wildlands League, <www.wildlands.org>, and World Wildlife Fund Canada, <www.wwfcanada.org>. (Thanks also to Angele Blasutti for making the maps of the Ancient Forest Water Trail.)

Thanks to all our family, friends, and Goulais River neighbours. We are especially appreciative to: Mom and Dad; Viv, Tim, Mirabai, and Fae; Irene, Rick, and family; Robin and Enn; Ruth and Gil; Ken and Rilla; Ruth and Ward; and Paul and Jane.

These are some, not all, of the people that we gratefully acknowledge for helping us during our journey: Bob Hansen and Nancy Chapman; Carmen at Kiosk; Ian, Lynda, Becky, and Sarah Kovacs; Dorothy Zimmerman; Peter and Marie Quinby; Tom Lee; John Kilbridge; Carin Colman and Francis Boyes; Leona. Thanks for a warm welcome at Bear Island, Lake Temagami: John Matchett and Alex and Mary Carol Mathias. And to the Taylor Statton campers we met en route, as well as Hugh Doran of Taylor Statton Camps and Harry Pearce of E. B. Eddy. And thanks to all the "Plauntation" families on Lake Pogamasing; Michael Bernier; Tarmo Poldmaa; Joan Foster; John Schreiber; Bob Collins; Louise Robillard and the Parks Canada folks at Fort St. Joseph National Historic Site; and all involved with MCTV-CTV's *Down to Earth* series: Paul Dempsey; Franco Mariotti; Dave Pearson; Mark Oldfield; and Bill Clegg.

We are also indebted to the following companies and individuals for assisting us with our unique telecommunications endeavour: Apple Canada, <www.apple.com>, Victor Chan, Christine Georgacopoulos, Ralph Kamuf and others; Art Osborne; Bell Global Solutions, Brian Allen; Eastman Kodak; Mobile Satellite Ventures, <www.msvlp.com>, Austin Comerton; NorthStar Computers, David Wheat and Julian Daniel; *Outdoor Photographer* and *PC Photo Magazine*, Christopher Robinson; Pictographics, <www.pictographics.com>, Luke and Desire Dalla Bona; and the *Sault Star*, Bob Richardson, John Halucha, and Bruno Vit.

We are forever grateful to Nissan Canada, <www.nissan.ca>, for helping us make the journey, the Web site, and post-journey projects possible. Thanks to Jacquie Adams, Brian Drennan, Susan Elliott, Frank Foggia, Jean-Luc Lemire, and Max Wickens. Thanks also to Sudbury Aviation, <www.sudburyaviation.on.ca>, Marg Watson and Mel Laidlaw.

Photography plays an essential role in our work in helping to protect Ontario's ancient forests. Our sincerest thanks to: Canon Canada, <www.canon.com>, Ian MacFarlane and Neil Stephenson; Fuji Photo Film Canada, <www.fujifilm.com>, Tim Berry; Stan C. Reade Photo, <www.stancreade.com>, Kieran Wallace; and DayMen Photo Marketing (Lowepro, Pelican, Slik), <www.daymen.com>, Michael Mayzel and Uwe Mummenhoff.

The comfort, safety, and enjoyment of day-to-day living on a long journey is dependent in part on one's knowledge and attitude. But great equipment, warm and waterproof clothing, and delicious food make it so much more so! Thanks to the following generous spirits who have faith in our projects: Mad River Canoe, <www.confluencewatersports.com>; DayMen Outdoor Marketing, <www.daymen.com> (Lowe Alpine, AlpineAire Foods, SmartWool), Bud Shirley, Helen Hughes, and others; Tilley Endurables, Alex Tilley; Loblaws Inc. (President's Choice products), Steve Brown; Rome's Independent Grocer, Steve and Kelly Rome; Grey Owl Paddles, Brian Dorfman; Tentsmiths, <www.tentsmiths.com>, Deborah and Peter Marques; Ostrom Outdoors, <www.ostrompacks.com>, Bill and Anne Ostrom; and Bugg Off, Carole Bradshaw.

And of course there would not be a book if it were not for McClelland & Stewart Publishers. We are indebted to you for your patience, good humour, faith, and unique perspective on the project. A final thanks to Doug Gibson, Nancy Grossman, Jonathan Webb, Elizabeth Kribs, Heather Sangster, and Kong.